BUDDHISM THROUGH
AMERICAN WOMEN'S EYES

BUDDHISM THROUGH AMERICAN WOMEN'S EYES

Edited by
Karma Lekshe Tsomo

Snow Lion Publications
Ithaca, New York

Snow Lion Publications
P. O. Box 6483
Ithaca, New York 14851 USA
607-273-8519

First edition USA 1995

Printed in the United States of America

ISBN 1-55939-047-6

Library of Congress Cataloging-in-Publication Data

Buddhism through American women's eyes / edited by Karma Lekshe Tsomo.
    p. cm.
  Includes bibliographical references and index.
  ISBN 1-55939-047-6
  1. Women—Religious life. 2. Religious life—Buddhism. 3. Buddhist
women—United States. I. Karma Lekshe Tsomo, Bhikṣuṇī, 1944-   .
BQ5450.B83 1995
294.3'082—dc20   95-10507
                                                                CIP

Table of Contents

Appreciation 7
Openings 9

1. Forging a Kind Heart in an Age of Alienation
   by Heidi Singh 15
2. Being Buddha *by Prabhasa Dharma* 25
3. Reflections on Impermanence: Buddhist Practice
   in the Emergency Room *by Margaret Coberly* 31
4. Mothering and Meditation *by Jacqueline Mandell* 47
5. Everyday Dharma *by Michelle Levey* 61
6. Bringing Dharma into Relationships *by Karuna Dharma* 71
7. Dealing with Stress *by Ayya Khema* 75
8. Abortion: A Respectful Meeting Ground *by Yvonne Rand* 85
9. Buddhism and the Twelve Steps *by Rachel V.* 90
10. Karma: Creative Responsibility *by Karma Lekshe Tsomo* 97
11. The Bodhisattva Peace Training *by Tsering Everest* 105
12. The Monastic Experience *by Karma Lekshe Tsomo, Eko
    Susan Noble, Furyu Schroeder, Nora Ling-yun Shih,
    and Jacqueline Mandell* 121
13. Eastern Traditions in Western Lands *by Eko Susan Noble* 149

Continuing the Conversation 155
Notes 161
Glossary 165
Further Reading 171
About the Contributors 175
Index 177

Dedication

Dedicated to all those teachers and practitioners striving to transmit the Buddha's teachings and adapt Buddhist practice to the North American setting in ways that are both comfortable and authentic.

Appreciation

The ancient Buddhist tradition of rejoicing in the merits of others is a skillful and enjoyable method of purifying jealousy and enhancing virtues. In the spirit of this magnanimous tradition, I deeply appreciate the wise and compassionate efforts of all the teachers represented in this volume and rejoice in the efforts of all those who prepare the way for North American women to discover Buddhism.

Warm thanks go to transcribers Trime Lhamo, Brittany Faulkner, Ulla Johnson, Travis McCauley, and the late Sandy Clark. Sandy is especially remembered for valiantly publicizing her struggle with AIDS for the benefit of other women. Heartfelt gratitude goes to Kimberly Snow, who created the Santa Barbara retreat from which this volume emerges, and to Lorena Cassady, Margaret Coberly, Donnë Florence, Ann Sturley, and Deb Moore for the warm encouragement they offered along with their skillful editorial suggestions.

Openings

The Buddha taught a useful path for human transformation and declared women and men equally capable of spiritual realization, yet most exemplars of this tradition throughout history have been men. Now that Buddhism is moving West and women are experiencing the teachings for themselves, with typical American pragmatism, they are interested in hearing firsthand the effects Buddhism has had on individual women's lives.

As Buddhism has gained popularity in their countries, Western people have naturally viewed the teachings through the lens of their own culture and psychology. Among the attractive features are Buddhism's experiential orientation, its pragmatic approach to spirituality, and its variety. The theory of human psychology based on personal responsibility fits well with Western individualism. The teachings on morality, compassion, and selfless service corroborate our own Judeo-Christian cultural heritage. The concept of karma, a law of cause and effect which extends to the mental and personal level, corresponds to the scientific principle of action and reaction in physics. And the common sense approach of Buddhist empiricism finds acceptance in the rational Western mind.

At the same time, there are elements that go against the grain of our cultural conditioning. Whereas the Buddha taught that happiness lies in limiting desires, American culture teaches that happiness can be found in fulfilling desires. While our culture teaches self-assertiveness and the pursuit of self-fulfillment, Buddhism teaches self-denial and other-centeredness. There is a tension between the otherworldiness of Buddhism and the this-worldliness of contemporary American life. Even within the Buddhist fold there is a tension between the relative values of study and meditation, a tension that has existed in every Buddhist society to date. Other problematic features emerge from Asian cultural carry-overs, such as hierarchical structures, authoritarianism, and sexism. There have been clashes between Eastern and Western psychological premises, between spiritual ideals and everyday realities, and especially between an egalitarian theory and women's actual roles in a traditionally patriarchal religion.

As Buddhism is transmitted to new environments, Western women are presented with a spiritual path in an Asian cultural package. They have felt a need to share experiences as they confront cultural differences between these ancient teachings and twentieth-century realities. At times, in addition to being spiritually enriching, Buddhist practice provides a window into different cultures. Buddhism, historically a bridge among cultures, has today become a bridge linking people of culturally diverse backgrounds worldwide. At other times, the cultural aspects, fascinating and colorful as they may be, are too alien or cumbersome to deal with. Many people go through cycles of enjoying and rejecting the cultural elements accompanying the Buddhist faith they have adopted. Yet, in the increasing globalization of Buddhism, Westerners, and especially Western women, are playing a major role.

Women in Buddhism receive mixed messages. In the Theravada texts, women's potential for achieving liberation is affirmed, yet in some of them women are denigrated as impediments to men's spiritual progress. In the Mahayana texts, women are said to have Buddha nature, the seed or potential to achieve perfect enlightenment, yet it is also said that women must become men before they can do that. The Vajrayana tradition affirms the possibility of highest enlightenment in a woman's body, yet almost all of its teachers are male. While women are assured in the traditional Buddhist texts that they have the highest potential, patriarchy is alive and well in the actual living traditions in Buddhist societies. Women may even have difficulty finding the requisites of the spiritual life. Understandably, then, Western women may feel confused when they see a contradiction between the rhetoric and the realities of these issues that concern their spiritual development. A grassroots Buddhist women's movement has been the natural result—the culmination of Western Buddhist women's responses to elements of sexism found in this otherwise attractive spiritual path.

The Buddha originally taught that enlightenment is possible for all beings, both human and non-human. He made it very clear that, within the human realm, women and men have an equal capacity for enlightenment. In Theravada countries such as Burma, Sri Lanka, and Thailand, enlightenment means liberation from samsara, the cycle of birth and rebirth. The Buddha maintained that women can achieve this liberation and during his lifetime thousands upon thousands of women did. We can still read the stories of their lives and their inspiring poems of spiritual insight.

In the Mahayana countries, enlightenment means achieving Buddhahood. One has to practice for many lifetimes to become a Buddha, but all living beings, women included, can and will. One example of a fully enlightened being in female form is Kuan Yin. Kuan Yin is one of the four female aspects of Avalokiteshvara, embodiment of compassion. Highly respected in China, Japan, Korea, and Vietnam, she sees the needs of sentient beings in all directions and leads them out of suffering.

In the Vajrayana tradition Tara, an embodiment of enlightened activity in female form, is called "the mother of all Buddhas." Tara accumulated merit in a woman's body for many lifetimes, purifying her mind and progressing along the paths and stages. When she was just about to achieve enlightenment, her Dharma friends told her to pray for a male rebirth since she would become a Buddha soon, but she refused. "Since many enlightened beings have appeared in male form," she vowed, "I shall manifest enlightenment in female form." She is called a liberator of beings and is a powerful symbol for Tibetans, who pray to her every day. Tara has twenty-one aspects, with different colors and gestures, each providing protection in a special area of life. Green Tara helps by providing good conditions for our spiritual practice, while White Tara blesses the practitioner with long life.

At the time of the Buddha, many achieved liberation by just hearing the teachings. Later, without the Buddha's presence, this achievement became progressively more difficult. Now the practice of Dharma has become extremely difficult and requires great effort. Even to aspire for spiritual development in this day and age is something very precious. Hundreds of activities and entertainments vie for our attention. Many temptations distract us from what is essential. And, seeking happiness, we naturally follow along. Unfortunately, our pleasure-seeking does not always bring us the happiness we expect and sometimes it leads us to grief. As a result, we experience a great deal of disappointment, dissatisfaction, and confusion within and around us. Very few have time to make spiritual practice their primary concern. Yet in order just to cope in a chaotic, stressful society, setting time aside for some kind of spiritual practice becomes essential.

The question of spiritual practice and its relation to everyday life situations arises again and again for Western Buddhists, with different teachers answering it different ways. The Buddha taught meditation as the cure for suffering, but how can we meditate when we are so confused? How can we take time to meditate when so many are suffering? How can we *find* time when our lives are so busy? Although one may believe in peace, kindness, and wisdom, manifesting these ideals in the world is not a simple or easy task.

Many women have been seeking opportunities to meet with other women practitioners, individually and in small groups, to learn from their experience. Discussion groups, whether organized or spontaneous, give women an opportunity to communicate intimately, and often profoundly, some of their ideas. Many find this kind of personal interaction and mutual encouragement extremely fruitful and strengthening. A caring approach, with openness of heart and a spirit of trust, enables us to talk about all aspects of our lives without risk of condemnation.

Western women, often highly educated, have access to Buddhist literature, yet soon discover how rare it is to find Buddhist teachings given by women! Patriarchal societies generally give far more attention, authority, and weight to men's words than to women's. Rarely have women been given the chance to air their understanding of the teachings. It is possible that women may interpret the Buddha's teachings in ways similar to men, but we shall never know unless we listen to them.

The words of the female elders (*theris*), so fortuitously documented, are practically the only record we have of women speaking from the heart about their Buddhist spiritual life. The *theris* were surely not the only women throughout 2600 years of Buddhist history to gain insights, yet of the others we have no record. And, as extremely valuable as these verses are for documenting Buddhist women's spiritual achievements, they are, after all, the words of women belonging to a very different time and culture than our own. Today's women want to hear from today's women, to whom they can easily relate.

Here, then, we give women a chance to express themselves on the Dharma and their experiences of adapting and implementing the teachings in their daily lives. Rejecting the preconception that women are only qualified to speak on women's issues, these experienced women practitioners discuss Buddhist philosophy, its contribution to world peace, its practical application to everyday life, and the practice of Buddhism in the Western world.

Chapter 1

Forging a Kind Heart in an Age of Alienation

by Heidi Singh

Those who lived in Los Angeles during the riots of 1982 will remember the alienation, mistrust, anger, frustration, and tremendous fear that permeated every segment of the community and
every level of society. Frustration was a major component of the
experience: a feeling of helplessness, coupled with an overwhelming depression over the present and anxiety concerning the future.
However, after the riots, after much contemplation and discussion
with friends and strangers, I was convinced that the principles of
reconciliation can be applied not only to our families, but to our
cities as well. The teachings of Buddhism are very clear about compassion as an antidote to alienation and anger, whether on the personal, civic, or global level.

There are two guiding principles found in the Buddhist scriptures which have tremendous importance for all practitioners. The
first is a segment of the twin verses of *The Dhammapada*:

> Hatred is never overcome by hatred;
> Hatred is overcome only by love.
> This is an eternal law.[1]

The second is contained in the *Karaniya Metta Sutta*, or *Discourse on
Loving Kindness*:

> As a mother would risk her own life
> To protect her only child,
> Even so let one cultivate a boundless heart
> Towards all living beings.
> Let one's love pervade the whole world,
> Without any obstructions,
> Above, below and across,
> Without hatred, without enmity.[2]

It was inspiring to me to discover that Venerable Maha Ghosananda, the beloved and respected monk and teacher, cites these two passages in a special prayer he composed for the peace of Cambodia and the world.[3] I also use these verses from the Tibetan tradition:

> With the determination to accomplish the highest welfare for all sentient beings, who excel even the wish-granting gem, may I at all times hold them dear!
>
> Whenever I associate with someone, may I think myself the lowest among all and hold the other supreme in the depth of my heart!
>
> In all actions may I search into my mind, and as soon as delusion arises, endangering myself and others, may I firmly face and avert it!
>
> When I see beings of wicked nature, pressed by violent sin and affliction, may I hold these rare ones dear as if I had found a precious treasure!
>
> When others, out of envy, treat me badly with abuse, slander and the like, may I suffer the defeat and offer the victory to others!
>
> When the one whom I have benefited with great hope hurts me very badly, may I behold him as my supreme Guru!
>
> In short, may I, directly and indirectly, offer benefit and happiness to all my mothers; may I secretly take upon myself the harm and suffering of the mothers!
>
> May all this remain undefiled by the stains of keeping in view the Eight Worldly Principles; may I, by perceiving all Dharmas as illusive, unattached, be delivered from the bondage of samsara![4]

These deceptively simple words are very difficult to fully understand, and even more difficult to put into practice. In 1972, when my husband and I were first married and living in India, His Holiness the Dalai Lama gave us a copy of this text. I have treasured this small booklet for the past twenty years and have pondered over it at many stages of my life. I am not sure I understand it even now, but I am convinced that it is a valuable teaching to put into practice and a worthy ideal to strive toward.

Meditation Practice

There is no doubt that the regular practice of meditation is a fundamental requisite for any kind of reconciliation. I doubt if one can attempt any real healing of relationships without it. Of course, psychotherapy is a great help, particularly in cases where one has been abused and/or is in a co-dependency situation. More and more, psychologists and psychiatrists have begun to see the value of meditation as a tool in dealing with family dynamics.

Personally, I am convinced that the reconciliation I have experienced with my parents could not have been possible without my meditation practice. This is particularly true in my relationship with my father, who passed away in March of 1991, and who was a lifelong alcoholic. A brief exploration of that relationship will illustrate the role of Buddhist practice in family reconciliation far better than any theoretical explication.

First, it is essential to point out the very important role of loving-kindness meditation in this process. My own teacher, Venerable Balangoda Anandamaitreya (who is now nearly ninety-eight years old), never ceases to emphasize the power and importance of this practice, particularly in personal relationships. Whenever I speak to him, he urges me most insistently to practice loving-kindness meditation toward my husband and especially toward my parents. Communication had previously been a missing aspect of my relationship with my father. Even when we spoke to each other, it was never on a heart level, but only about superficial matters. Although the situation looked particularly hopeless with regard to my father, Venerable Anandamaitreya assured me that if I practiced loving-kindness toward my father every day at the same time, without fail, things would improve.

An Unexpected Result

Just a few months after my teacher's instruction, after he had returned to Sri Lanka, my family suddenly learned that my father was very sick. Indeed, he was dying of lung cancer that had metastasized to his bones, a fact which he had known for some time but had hidden from me, my mother, my husband and son. By the time I discovered his secret, my father was entering the final stages of his life. In the end there remained only one week to say our good-byes and come to an understanding.

A major breakthrough had occurred about twelve days before my father passed away. I was visiting my father in a regular ward of the VA Hospital in Los Angeles. He was angry as usual, at everything and everyone *except* me, it seemed. He suddenly turned to me and said with eyes glassy from unrelenting pain and an ever-increasing dosage of powerful drugs, "The thing I can't understand is, why me? I've never hurt anyone in my entire life!"

Of course, I was dumbfounded and had to take a moment to collect my thoughts. How could I reply to this? My immediate reaction in the past would have been anger. Here was a man who had caused endless pain to a great many people during his lifetime, particularly my mother and me. How could he possibly claim he had never hurt anyone? At the time, however, I realized that he was gravely ill, though I did not yet fully understand that he was dying. I knew that retaliation on my part would not be helpful, either to him or to me. Another route was available to me: to play the co-dependent role of "Mary Sunshine," a lifelong learned pattern of behavior. This would enable my father to indulge his self-pity, while assuring him that indeed he had done nothing to hurt anyone and didn't deserve his suffering.

At that moment, however, I chose a middle path. I was honest with my father for perhaps the first time in my life. I took a deep breath and said in a very calm voice, "Dad, I don't think it has anything to do with that. Everyone is subject to suffering and illness. We are all vulnerable to disease. This is just part of being human." He looked at me quietly, with a little surprise. He seemed calmer than before. This was the first episode in a whole series of events that paved the way for our reconciliation.

On his sixty-seventh birthday, my father was moved out of the regular ward and into a hospice a few floors down. A long conversation with the hospice director helped me deal with the shock of what was happening. Just the night before, my father had telephoned me, raving about an operation the doctors could perform that would be his last chance. His being so out of touch with reality is not uncommon among terminally ill patients, who sometimes grasp at straws for any hope of recovery. My confusion was compounded by my father's lifelong tendency to fantasize and fabricate a whole reality of his own. The hospice director assured me that my father knew he was dying and had made the decision to enter the hospice himself. She added, however, that he could use my support to bolster his decision.

That evening, my husband, my young son, and I visited my Dad in the hospice to celebrate in a quiet way his last birthday. In the days ahead, there was much to do. My father communicated a sense of urgency and asked me to take care of some personal matters for him. I also called my mother in Sacramento immediately and told her gently that if she wanted to say good-bye to my Dad, she should come right away. Although my parents had been divorced for twenty years, my father was my mother's first and only true love, in spite of all the suffering their marriage caused her.

Thus, my mother and I were able to be with my father in his final days. Looking back, my great regret is that, being overwhelmed with practical matters at the time, I did not have the opportunity to be completely reflective about the tremendous event that was taking place. Nevertheless, whenever I had the chance, usually late at night, I meditated and prayed and considered how best to help my father through the transition he was about to undergo. It was at this time that I sought help from a small volume that a Zen monk friend had given me about fifteen years earlier: Philip Kapleau's *The Wheel of Death*.[5] In this small and clear book, I found the necessary strength and assistance to prepare for my father's death. Particularly helpful to me were the ten (Mahayana) precepts as formulated in the section entitled "Dying: Practical Instructions":

I resolve not to kill but to cherish all life.

I resolve not to take what is not given but to respect the things of others.

I resolve not to engage in improper sexuality but to practice purity of mind and self-restraint.

I resolve not to lie but to speak the truth.

I resolve not to cause others to use liquors or drugs which confuse or weaken the mind, nor to do so myself, but to keep my mind clear.

I resolve not to speak of the misdeeds of others but to be understanding and sympathetic.

I resolve neither to praise myself nor to condemn others but to overcome my own shortcomings.

I resolve not to withhold spiritual or material aid but to give it freely where needed.

I resolve not to become angry but to exercise control.

I resolve not to revile the Three Treasures [i.e., the Buddha, the Dharma, and the Sangha] but to cherish and uphold them.[6]

These were my guiding principles as I recited the *Heart Sutra* and prepared daily for the task of being with my father and comforting him as all of us awaited the momentous imminent event.

During this time, my compassion toward my father grew, and I began to see him as a being whose whole life, since his early childhood, had been eaten up by suffering. This suffering caused him to lash out at others and cause more pain in a cycle that he did not understand and was therefore powerless to stop. The time for recriminations and judgment on my part had long passed. I realized that the task at hand was to help my father die with as peaceful a heart as possible.

Another thing that happened was that I was finally able to feel a deep love for my father that had long been dormant in my heart due to abandonment and fear of rejection. This was the great gift of non-fear that I derived from the recitation of the *Heart Sutra.*[7] This was the fearlessness I needed to see my father through the great passage which all humans fear above all else.

The Last Day

Spiritually, my Dad was in pretty good shape. He had been visited regularly by the Catholic chaplains of the hospital and had received the last rites more than once. The day before he died, my mother and I had brought a priest friend to see him as well. That was fortunate, because this same priest would be the celebrant of my father's funeral Mass. I brought my father some small prayer books and a new rosary because he had lost his old one. But nevertheless, I knew my father was feeling afraid and alone.

The day he died, a strange thing happened. My father emphatically refused all medication. It seemed he was very determined to have a clear mind when he made his transition. That morning, when I went to see him alone, the sight of his physical condition was appalling. His body was shrunken and his face was emaciated. He looked like a corpse already, although he was fully conscious. I felt helpless. I did not want to do anything to upset him or cause him more pain. Gently, I spoke to him and touched his arm. He was glad I was there, but could no longer speak.

Finally, I asked him if I could recite a Buddhist prayer for him. I still don't know why I asked this, but I knew it was more for me than for him. He nodded somewhat enthusiastically, so slowly and calmly I recited the *Heart Sutra* near his ear. To my surprise, as I was reciting, he kept his eyes closed and tears streamed down his face.

When I finished, I suddenly felt an outpouring of love for my father, along with the courage to unlock my tongue and tell him all the things I could never say before. Here he was a captive, and the gift of non-fear exercised itself in me. Gently I told him how much I loved him and that I was grateful to him for all the good things he had done for me. I reassured him that I would pray for him always and do whatever I could for him. Tears continued to stream down his face. Fearing that I was upsetting him, I asked him if he wanted me to leave. He shook his head emphatically, "No." Then I asked him if he wanted me to stop talking. He nodded, "Yes." And so, silently, I stood by him for some time and mentally did the loving-kindness and healing meditation that I had been doing for him every day.

After awhile, I told him that I had to leave but would be back soon. I brought my mother and son to the hospital to see him in the afternoon. Then, knowing my husband wanted to say goodbye, I picked him up and we all returned to the hospital. My husband and son talked to him, and my husband took our son out to the car after a few minutes. My mother and I remained, somewhat confused and anxious. We looked at each other helplessly. My father's death seemed imminent and we did not want to leave him alone, yet we could not possibly know exactly when it would occur.

Suddenly, just before eight o'clock, my father sat up in his bed with a great struggle. Instantly we knew he was dying. He looked at us with eyes wide open, though by now his sight was gone, and tried desperately to speak. Both my mother and I were somewhat awestruck by the enormity of what was happening and by the sudden energy with which my father was urgently trying to communicate. Yet both of us stood our ground and gently but very firmly talked to him. We reassured him that we loved him and that we would stand by him and pray for him. Somewhat impulsively, I told my Dad that he had nothing to worry about and not to be afraid. For the first time, he was going to be really happy. Over and over, my Mom and I just told him gently that we loved him. I also told him that nothing remained undone. He could not speak, but he opened his mouth and mouthed the words, "I love you." And after a few minutes of struggle, he lay back down on his pillow, closed his eyes, and after a few more breaths, with some difficulty, died. He had been just eight days in the hospice.

Reconciliation and Daily Practice

In the days and weeks following my father's death, I wholeheartedly did the practice outlined in *The Wheel of Death*, reciting the ten precepts and the prayer suggested by Philip Kapleau, followed by the *Heart Sutra*, and the bodhisattva vows.[8] In the week after his death, we had several services for my father, including a Catholic Mass (where I gave the eulogy), a Buddhist service at my temple, and a full military funeral at the VA cemetery. Several Buddhist monks conducted services and we observed the forty-ninth day after death. There was a special service at the temple on the ninetieth day, in accordance with Sri Lankan custom. My husband and his family in India offered prayers in the Sikh tradition, and Hindu friends and relatives also did puja for him.

For me personally, the reality of my father's death intensified and deepened my own practice, particularly through the recitations that I was making on his behalf. The first days after his death, I was especially intent on helping him make the transition in whatever way I could and reassuring him that we were all doing our best to help him through. The precise instructions given to me by my revered teacher and those few months of intense practice had prepared me, though I had had no idea what I was preparing for.

Looking back, I see that the road to reconciliation had been paved by my own acceptance of my father. In the previous year and a half, we had resumed contact. I had accepted his strange visits and gifts without rancor and had made the effort to get together for happy, if somewhat tense, celebrations of birthdays and holidays. He had made a great deal of effort to meet me, too, and only after his death did I realize the urgency with which he had approached these get-togethers. I regret not knowing that he was dying. Yet my acceptance of my father was probably that much sweeter to him, precisely because I didn't know.

Bloomfield and Felder, in their book *Making Peace with Your Parents*, sum up the most compelling argument for attempting reconciliation:

> To make peace with your parents, you may have to give up a lot. You may have to give up your resentments, your anger, your annoyance, your desire to punish and your need to blame. You may have to give up resisting your parents and be prepared even for times when it appears that they win and you lose. You may have to learn to admire and respect a parent for whom you may now feel a degree of contempt and hate. Indeed, you may need to learn to accept your parents exactly the way they are rather than the way you think they should be.

"Why bother?" or "Who cares?" you might say. It is not primarily for your parents, but for you. Your peace of mind, your love and work relationships, and your moment-to-moment aliveness may be at stake.[9]

There are many ways to go about the work of reconciliation. Getting in touch with your anger is one approach, but it isn't enough. Indeed, as Thich Nhat Hanh observes, we need to get to the roots of our anger and achieve real transformation through understanding and mindfulness.[10] Thich Nhat Hanh also claims, in a way that touches me deeply, that true reconciliation can be developed through the development of true compassion:

> We can also meditate on the suffering of those who cause us to suffer. Anyone who has made us suffer is undoubtedly suffering too. We only need to follow our breathing and look deeply, and naturally we will see his suffering. A part of his difficulties and sorrows may have been brought about by his parents' lack of skill when he was still young. But his parents themselves may have

been victims of their parents; the suffering has been transmitted from generation to generation and been reborn in him. If we see that, we will no longer blame him for making us suffer, because we know that he is also a victim. To look deeply is to understand. Once we understand the reasons he has acted badly, our bitterness towards him will vanish, and we will long for him to suffer less. We will feel cool and light, and we can smile. We do not need the other person to be present in order to bring about reconciliation. When we look deeply, we become reconciled with ourselves, and, for us, the problem no longer exists. Sooner or later, he will see our attitude and will share in the freshness of the stream of love which is flowing naturally from our heart.[11]

For me, reconciliation would not have been possible without all the components that make up my practice: meditation, recitation and chanting, study, and the observance of precepts. They all go together toward forging a kind and compassionate heart, which we want to achieve. And these components of practice pave the way to liberation for all beings, for in liberating ourselves from anger, hatred, and ignorance, we help liberate from their suffering a great many others, especially those beings with whom we have an immediate karmic connection.

Just weeks after my father's passing, the abbot of my temple called and asked if I would be willing to observe the traditional eight precepts permanently. When he explained them in detail, I said, "No problem." I also expressed a wish to add a few. Working with three eminent Sri Lankan scholar-monks, we developed a new ministerial ordination utilizing twelve precepts and emphasizing the long-standing bodhisattva path in the Theravada tradition that has been overlooked in the past. During the celebration of Vesak in 1991, I was ordained as a bodhichari along with two others at our temple in Los Angeles. My ordination, I believe, was my father's gift to me. As the *Shobogenzo* says:

> By accepting and upholding the precepts in your deepest heart you can eventually attain to supreme enlightenment.... Who could possibly reject this? Buddhas have shown to countless living beings that when they wholeheartedly take into their life the moral precepts they do in time attain Buddhahood, becoming Perfectly Enlightened.... The wind and fire [the inner energies] fanned by the profound influence of Buddhas [as a result of accepting the precepts] drive one into the intimacy of enlightenment. This is the awakening of the wisdom mind.[12]

Chapter 2
Being Buddha

by Prabhasa Dharma

What is the nature of relationships in Buddhism? On the one hand, we can say that we are always in proper relationship. Shakyamuni Buddha realized this when he saw the true nature of the universe—the ongoing process of correct relationships among things. Through meditation we are able to leave the dimension of discursive thinking and enter a realm that is beyond description and conception. This is the realization of the underlying truth, the *dharmakaya*, or "truth body." Having realized this, we begin to shift away from identifying with the world of objects, particularly the body, which is highly perishable and ephemeral. We identify instead with the true essence body and its true activities. False imaginings and projections are dispelled, and harmonious relations ensue.

The German word for imagination is *forstellen*, which means "to project something before you that is not actually there." Most of us create projections between ourselves and what actually is. Through sitting meditation, the Buddha found that we can completely dispel these projections and relax into ultimate truth. Thus we realize the dharmakaya that functions perfectly. With this realization, we can put down all our worries, anxieties, and fears, and begin to enjoy who we really are, maybe for the first time. We do this without criticizing ourselves or changing anything, at least for that moment.

The consciousness that discerns things changes from moment to moment. In this vast and spacious openness, everything is possible. We are back in the world of form—with its cities, mountains, and deserts—experiencing the movement and feelings of this constantly changing body/mind complex. These things are not apart from ultimate reality, but simultaneous.

Traveling so much, I realize more and more the truth of what the Buddha meant when he said everything is like a dream. Moving around also makes me realize how impermanent and transparent this objective world is, as well as how interconnected we all are.

Sometimes my life is hectic, as I fly around the world on Dharma business. The difference between me and the business manager sitting next to me on the plane is that I have a refuge within and can sit in that quiet silent place. I feel connected with all the houses and people passing below, because each individual is a manifestation of the total principle. We are linked with everything, moment to moment. What each individual does affects the whole. This is the Buddha's teaching on dependent origination, that factors constantly interact and mutually penetrate. As we say in Zen, "When a cow is fed in China, a horse is satisfied in India."

In Buddhism we don't speak much about miracles; the miracle is every moment of everyday life. Miracles happen every day; we don't walk on water, but we fly through the air. The mind is dynamically at work, while the unborn and uncreated is beyond human conception. These are the two principles of one truth.

A simple formula for handling relationships is to remember that in principle, we are always one, though in the world of form, we are also different. Problems arise when this truth is not lived. That is why we need to realize the mind itself, through meditation, the great therapy of Buddha Shakyamuni. Meditation can help us be completely present to the situation and the needs of our neighbors, families, and friends.

The wonderful part is that there is nothing to be done and nothing to be achieved. From this very moment, we can enjoy just being here. When we simply sit and let go of doing, we see that we are in correct relationship with the whole universe. There is no "I" breathing—there is just breathing. Being silent, we don't have to worry about any relationship. Not being "self," we don't have to worry about anything at all.

There are Catholic priests and nuns among my students in Europe. Sometimes I choose words from my Christian background, like "peace on earth and good will to all." I tell them, "I am not here to make you Buddhists; you are Buddhas already. We don't need to discard the terms, just understand them correctly. To be a Buddha means to be awake." By the very nature of the Dharma, we are all spiritual beings, even those who believe themselves to be atheists. There is a sutra that says the bodhisattva Avalokiteshvara (Kuan Yin or Kannon), through her deeds, reveals the best in each being. We can take this simple phrase and make it the guideline of our life. Thus we meet Buddha all the time.

From the perspective of ultimate truth, the things we do in the relative world, the world of form, suddenly look very funny to us. After the intensive meditation of a sesshin, beginners often ask, "Now that we are going back to the *real* world, what should we do?" But the world is nothing other than each person's mental perception of what is going on. Whatever I say or do reflects the state of my consciousness and how I perceive the immense complexity of a given event. When we meditate, we get some first-hand experience of reality that enables us to transform the world around us.

When speaking of relationships, the safest thing to relate to is always Buddha. The one who is discriminating is myself. We can address every being we meet—not only human beings but also animals—as essentially Buddha. We talk with Buddha, eat with Buddha, drink with Buddha, go to sleep with Buddha, and wake up with Buddha. In Western terms, we speak of being in the presence of God or meeting God all the time. In the phenomenal world, we make a shift from self-centeredness, where we are constantly defending ourselves, to realizing there is nothing but Buddha or mind. Everybody defends their own ideas, perceptions, or projections, but the words themselves have no intrinsic reality. People fight about the meaning of God or Buddha, of "this" or "that," but how far does it get us?

When we begin to live in the reality that all beings are Buddha or God or whatever we name this highest principle, we are never out of proper relationship. Though many people in the world believe otherwise, we can never be not-Buddha. The Buddhist way is not to convert, but to raise the consciousness of others by our own deeds. When our minds are at peace, everything in the world works correctly. The sun and moon have never been out of order; things just get shuffled up a bit sometimes, because of our misdeeds. This doesn't mean that we turn away from the world. Rather, we develop the correct view, understanding that things are here for just a brief moment and then they are gone. The whole world we perceived and just talked about is already past, so what is the use of fighting over it? Indeed, we should just smile and enjoy being in the presence of all these Buddhas. If some are a little confused or stuck somewhere, the kind thing is not to blame or punish, but to help them get free.

The youngest member of our Institute is now one year old and he truly meditates. When he was still in his mother's tummy, he was sitting with her. When the mother was in labor, the doctor said, "We are going to have to turn this baby around, because he's sitting up in you." Just minutes later, as if he had heard the words, the baby suddenly made a somersault and turned around. He came out just at the right time. I gave the mother the "Om mani padme hum" mantra to chant, and a melodious way to chant it. After the baby was born, I told him, "You might as well be happy, because the alternative is to be unhappy, and who wants to be unhappy? You might as well be kind, because the alternative is to be unkind, and who wants to be unkind? You might as well be peaceful, because the alternative is to be angry, and who wants to be angry?"

We can say the same thing to ourselves. We might as well be happy, because the alternative is to be unhappy. We might as well be friendly, because the alternative is to be unfriendly. When we are kind to others, laughing and joyful, we are doing the best service to ourselves. Our energy and patience grow and we are able to affirm others. There is nothing else to learn or teach. The result of all the struggles we go through in meditation is to *be* love. That is actually what every religion teaches.

We begin by accepting, maybe by way of faith, that ultimately our mind is Buddha mind. We take a step: from now on, I am causing love. I am causing correct relationship. We remain completely open toward all. Our attitude of being loving and kind extends to all beings, including inanimate objects. I proclaim myself to be a secret agent. Standing in line at the post office, I do my secret agent job: radiating good feelings towards everyone, just standing there smiling and being at peace with myself. Relaxing into the knowledge that everything is already OK suddenly makes the people around you OK, too.

When we are in a state of being Buddha, we are not reactive toward others, but always act from knowledge, realization, and inner truth. Buddha is mind, free from conditioning. The pristine mind, inner freedom, is our true state. Since all things return to zero, in which they are equalized, we can also say that Buddha is the equalizer. We can look at the whole world of technology, philosophy, psychology, science, and begin to make the very interesting discovery that nothing in the whole world of human endeavor functions outside that principle. All the things we have invented are just manifestations of that one principle. Every moment throughout the whole universe is returning to this pristine state, to this unconditioned mind. Then a new arising happens—what we call a new moment, a new happening, a new encounter, a new relationship.

This principle is like a car with a stick shift. We have to go through neutral to change gears. We have to be empty of third gear before going into fourth. Similarly, our mind is empty of own-being. When we realize this, we can never be insulted or hurt. As the Buddha said, "When nobody is home, you cannot deliver a gift." The insults and hurts find no recipient, no target, when there is no one there to defend.

We always let people get to us. We spend enormous quantities of energy in defensiveness. Like somebody in a dream, we splash madly around, when there's nobody there. To realize our innate true nature, we must first realize our sameness: in that nature of no-form, we are all the same. Because the mind is empty, we can do anything we want. The problem is that we use the mind wrongly; instead, we must use it correctly.

Of course, this is easier said than done. It has been taught for more than two thousand years, but just hearing it is not the solution. We need an individual practice—a discipline.

The Buddhist way, particularly Zen, is very simple, straightforward, and individual. In a room, we see fifty people sitting together in meditation posture, and we assume that they are all doing the same thing. But because people are very different and are at different levels of realization, each one of us has a different practice.

Discarding our knowledge, we remain empty and open, which is our true state of consciousness, "the mirror mind." Realizing the dharmakaya, the "truth body," we let the empty mind return to its natural state. Everything appears before the mirror mind just as it is, not altered or distorted in any way. As we live the Buddhist wisdom, the world and everything in it changes. Gone are the dualistic ways of thinking, with this side and that side. Our deep realization of everything being Buddha "as it is" can also evoke a change of consciousness in others. We realize this Buddha nature, which we all have, that is free and not fixed in any form. We realize the fluid nature of the mind that has no problem. Why waste time being otherwise? We can save ourselves a lot of pain and strain.

Buddha mind is one, so in essence, we are the same. And Buddha mind, as the absolute aspect, has no karma. When we live in the absolute aspect, we create no karma. But when we get stuck in the physical aspect and take it to be real, we make all sorts of karma on the phenomenal, apparent level. Our karmic dispositions are different and are always changing, but the eye of truth sees beyond all distinctions, by direct intuition. It sees the suchness of the moment.

Once two Zen priests in Japan went to visit an artist. The artist had just finished a modern brush painting, so he asked the two Zen priests to inscribe it. The priests were a bit puzzled. The picture was so abstract, they didn't know what to write. They turned it this way and that, trying to figure out what it was. Finally one of them wrote, "It appears to be a horse," and the other one wrote, "...so it seems."

Our world is like that. It appears that we have this karma...so it seems. When we realize that it is not really there, we can drop it like old baggage and not create any more. We cannot be entirely free from the effects of karma created in the past; that has to spin itself out. But when we know that there is no real self, even when we suffer some pain, we see it ultimately as an illusion. Check it out. We live every moment completely aware and don't create more karma. We see all beings as Buddha.

Chapter 3

Reflections on Impermanence: Buddhist Practice in the Emergency Room

by Margaret Coberly

The distance that the dead have gone
  Does not at first appear—
Their coming back seems possible
  For many an ardent year.

—*Emily Dickinson*

Since human life in the Kali Yuga
  is brief and uncertain,
It would be regrettable to squander
  it in meaningless activity.

—*Gampopa*

In 1975, after deciding to specialize in emergency nursing, I started to work in a very large inner-city trauma center in New York's Spanish Harlem. The death scene occurred daily, sometimes three or four times a day. Family members were left devastated and sobbing in the crowded corridor, invariably ignored by the hospital staff. Everyone was too busy performing CPR or suturing a gaping wound to risk getting involved in the family psycho-social process surrounding death. Few caregivers knew what to say, anyway. "People die everyday. We do our best to save lives. Some don't make it. What can I say?" the physician asks defensively.

When holding and consoling a tormented, grieving person, the most difficult part is to remain objective. While maintaining an empathetic response to the situation, the compassionate caregiver must learn how to be an integral, essential part of the crisis situation and yet remain unattached to the outcome. One scenario that comes vividly to mind is the following. A young drug dealer involved in a cocaine robbery was brought to the emergency room with a gunshot wound to the right chest wall. While I was in the trauma room helping to stabilize this patient, another code trauma was announced and a woman receiving cardiopulmonary resuscitation from two firefighters was rushed into the emergency operating room. She had sustained a lethal blow that lacerated her internally. Apparently her daughter, in a rage, had plunged a large, open pair of scissors into her back. The mother had already virtually bled to death, but valiant efforts to save her continued for another hour. A short time later, the daughter, who had overdosed, was wheeled into the emergency department and assigned to my area.

I began to feel uneasy when I realized that I would have to be the one to tell this girl when she regained consciousness that her mother was dead. I had just inserted a tube into her stomach preparing to wash out any residual pill particles that might remain undigested when suddenly another aspect of the drama began to unfold. I heard frantic family members loudly arguing and swearing in the waiting room. The story slowly began to unravel from within the hysterical reports. Apparently the mother had shot the young cocaine dealer, who was also her daughter's boyfriend. The daughter in retaliation had plunged the scissors into her mother's back, and believing that her boyfriend was dead, had then overdosed on Tuinal (a sleeping pill). In the emergency room, the boyfriend was stabilized and sent to the intensive care unit. The mother's corpse lay silent and cold in the sterile operating room. The detectives and police had to finish their reports on the suspected homicide before the coroner could transport the body to the city morgue. The daughter, beginning to respond to stimuli, was groaning and calling out in Spanish for her boyfriend.

Being very disquieted by the chaotic nature of this violent emotional situation surrounding death, I was relying heavily on hopes that the boyfriend had survived and was using this as consolation in telling the daughter that her mother had died. Though hours had passed, the girl was still groggy, confused, and hysterical. Unable to comprehend all the social and legal repercussions developing because of her actions, she sobbed in my arms. She couldn't identify herself as the angry daughter anymore, yet she had killed her own mother. Her life seemed meaningless to her except for the survival of the boyfriend. Listening to her, I realized how a death can suddenly induce recognition of the impermanence that pervades all existence. Concepts, heretofore unshakeably solid, unravel quickly when an awareness of death is born. It all happens very fast.

A deeply felt recognition of impermanence causes uneasiness and a disquieting sense of insecurity. We want something permanent to hold on to. This uncomfortable feeling leads one to search in the external world for someone or something to replace the devastating sense of internal loss. When not preoccupied with people, places, or things in the external world, a person is faced with being alone. The experience of profound aloneness can be spellbinding for a few, but strikes terror in the hearts of most. In this story, the boyfriend died in the intensive care unit and the girl, diagnosed as a suicidal risk, was committed to the psychiatric lockup unit.

In our culture, we are so unaccustomed to directly confronting the issues stemming from our mortality that we try to dull the sting of recognition when they surface. Far from understanding the positive value of exploring the subject of death, we tend to anesthetize ourselves with alcohol or drugs, to dull the normal grieving process. It is difficult to accept that we lack control over our ultimate fate. When someone dies it is a profoundly moving reality. Nobody can do anything to reverse the finality of death. I was forced to look at my own fear of death. When I objectively realized the absolute inevitability of death for everything and everyone, my reaction was not unlike that of most others—terror. How could life be so fragile, with only just a few breaths between life and death? During this time of inquiry into the relationship of death to life, I read *Universal Responsibility and the Good Heart* by the current Dalai Lama, and was irrevocably stunned by a statement he made:

> Since things do not exist just of their own accord, but in dependence on conditions, they change whenever they encounter different conditions. Thus, they come into existence in dependence on conditions and they cease in dependence on conditions. That very lack of any intrinsic existence, independent of cause and conditions, is the basis for all the changes that are possible in a phenomenon, such as birth, cessation and so forth.[1]

From this perspective, what we call death—death of even the smallest, most inanimate thing—can be seen as just one manifestation of the constantly changing nature of the universe. Many Westerners are uninformed or unaware of such a transpersonal perspective even when experiencing it themselves at some less conscious level. The transpersonal perspective on death and dying, however, is firmly rooted in Buddhism.

One experience I had in the trauma room gave me a sudden and vivid insight into the bigger picture—an expanded recognition which went beyond conventional thought and reflected the transient nature of all things. Surgeons were working on a multiple trauma victim trying to suture an oozing hole in the patient's aorta, while I performed open cardiac massage. I held the heart in the palm of one hand, pressing and releasing the ventricles with the other, simulating the intermittent contractions necessary to circulate the blood through the organism. Everything became one to me in that moment—life, death, and the heartbeat that separated the two, which I literally held between my hands. I realized with great intensity that people, preoccupied with the way they believe things are or should be, often overlook what is actually happening in the present moment. In the absence of preconceived ideas or expectations, every moment carries with it the potential for a fresh and new experience of the eternally changing kaleidescope of existence.

All who suffer serious injury, illness, loss, or the threat of death are jolted into a situation that suddenly is very tenuous. Longevity can no longer be taken for granted. This recognition shocks the habitual patterns of thought an individual has developed to characterize reality. Having one's fixed, structured conceptualizations and expectations suddenly threatened by death, however, can lead to deep insights into the impermanent nature of all phenomena. Often this insight leads to a healthy sense of freedom from the overwhelming fear usually accompanying death. To be with a dying person is to recognize that separation is inevitable. Separation can occur at any time and this recognition continually challenges one's sense of permanence. Being compassionate and empathetic with a dying person can promote an intensely moving and profound interaction: the underlying awareness that each day could be the last is a powerful antidote to superficial chatter and pretentious interactions. Reality becomes what is happening right now— in the present one moment that might be the last. What has gone before no longer exists; what is to come is only fantasy. In the face of preconceived ideas involvement in the dying process can transform one's habitual, mundane pattern of existence to a life infused with the sacredness of all existence.

The greater visibility of the Fourteenth Dalai Lama, Tenzin Gyatso, since his exile from Tibet in 1959 and his recent award of the Nobel Peace Prize, along with an increasing number of publications by Tibetan teachers and scholars, has contributed to the growing public awareness of Tibet and its richly detailed psychological teachings. I found in these teachings an abundant source of information regarding death, dying and impermanence.

The Tibetan Buddhist view of death is remarkable in many ways, especially in that it maintains that an innate wakefulness or awareness of our true inner nature—the light within—is potentially present in all of us. The now-famous Evans-Wentz translation of *The Tibetan Book of the Dead* contains the message that a person, dead or alive, has a choice in any given moment to transform his or her perceptions of reality from externalized to internalized sources. Tibetan Buddhist doctrine maintains that this transformation can occur by recognizing the transitory nature of the universe— impermanence. Recognizing the impermanent nature of the universe enables a person to see through habitual patterns of thinking to the importance of the present moment. In one sense, this realization that the present moment is the only reality that truly exists involves letting go of the past as well as of preconceptions about the future.

I had been confronted by death almost every day as a nurse in an inner-city emergency room in Los Angeles. Many of us there cried at times; but we did not talk about death. Life seemed impermanent around death, uncertain and insecure, especially when a child died—but there was never time for discussion, and we knew well how to work in that emergency room as though death were quite distant from us all. Thus, I was not prepared for experiencing a personal death in my own family.

Waiting in the thoracic surgeon's office for my brother Wheeler's diagnosis, I felt emotionally paralyzed. The room vibrated with tension and fear and I could almost feel the second hand dragging itself across the face of my watch, stalking the moments, as we waited for the news. Wheeler was scared, and so was I. It was difficult for me to look at him. Rather than face him, and confront questions about his possible death, I concentrated on three rows of dusty, antique chemistry bottles in a cabinet behind the surgeon's desk. Examining those old bottles I tried to subdue the terror and panic rising inside me. The physician came in briskly, slid the x-rays onto the view boxes, and flipped the lights on behind each one. Pointing to a large, irregular form in the thoracic cavity depicted on the film, he summarized—distantly and technically—a few possible causes for the large and ominous shadow. He ended his constrained explanation by declaring: "It has to be considered malignant until proven otherwise." A seeming eternity of screamingly silent moments passed as we stared at the M.D. in stunned disbelief. Then we started asking questions rapidly, searching for some small thread of error in the situation. After all, how could someone so youthful, successful, intelligent, handsome and well-loved as Wheeler have a terminal illness? It just could not be true. Denial was the only coping mechanism we had available for this unanticipated and unwelcome turn of events.

The terminal diagnosis is a major turning point in the life of a patient and his or her significant others. Routine ways of thinking and living are suddenly and violently interrupted. But certainty is nowhere to be found, and denial is often the first response to this sudden and alarming exposure to impermanence.

The Tibetan Buddhist approach is to cultivate mindfulness of death every day of life for the primary purpose of gaining insight into the impermanent nature of the universe. Tibetan Buddhism asserts that an awareness of the transient quality of life expands one's mental outlook by enhancing concern for the welfare of others, deepening an appreciation for the present moment, and greatly reducing the fear of death. One important Tibetan Buddhist method suggested for cultivating an awareness of death involves meditating daily on the following three ideas:

(1) Death is definite: death has come to everyone in the past; there is no way to halt the passing of our time; and everything is subject to change and therefore impermanent.

(2) The time of death is indefinite: human life has no definite life span; the chances for death are great; and the human body is frail.

(3) At the time of death nothing else matters except one's mental state: friends and relatives are of no help; wealth or power cannot help; and the body cannot help.

I took care of Wheeler for three months while he was dying of cancer in his home. Although we had always been extremely close, we became intractably bonded during the process of his dying. We worked very hard together to try to maintain a level of objective understanding about death so that Wheeler could experience the radiance of an individual who has found peace within himself. Whether a patient, a loved one, or a caregiver, any person who is at ease around terminal illness and death can give immeasurable comfort to family and friends who are frightened and confused about the imminence of death. There is no way to eradicate the grief and sadness that accompany death; stripped of fear, however, death can be a moment of intense unity between all those present. The last few breaths my brother took were moments suspended in time. Whispering reassuringly to him, and holding his head on my arm, I struggled with having to let go of him as he passed out of his ravaged body forever. The finality of death is dazzling in its clarity. The sense of loss I felt was excruciatingly painful and yet looking at Wheeler's corpse, I realized that the part of me observing death was precisely the same thing that had just departed from his body.

During the last three months of Wheeler's life, he had become increasingly interested in spiritual matters. We read together a book called *Advice from a Spiritual Friend* written by Geshe Rabten and Geshe Dhargyey. This powerfully simple, clear and profound book states unequivocally the Buddhist concept that learning to be happy and content in any circumstance depends upon our attitude both towards ourselves and others. The quintessential advice it contains is from the Buddhist tradition as upheld in Tibet. The Tibetans have preserved a rich tradition of lore concerning death and dying, most of it containing practical, sensible methods with which to develop an understanding about death, the future evolution of the mind, and thus about life. A Westerner might reasonably ask, "How can there be a future evolution for the mind when the body dies?" In the Buddhist view the idea of rebirth is fundamental; before this life, each of us has died many deaths. Birth and death are two sides of the same coin. According to this view, realization can be experienced directly through the practice of deep concentration and meditation, during which the subconscious memory stores of past experience can be tapped.

Tibetan Buddhism claims that a human being, by redirecting his or her motivation, or intention, can ultimately evolve to a state of awareness that enables liberation from a long succession of rebirths. Every lifetime is but a transient intermediate state, the conditions of which are dependent on the actions that have preceded it, just as the conditions of future rebirth are dependent on the actions of today. Recognizing that life can change at any moment, and that the time of death is uncertain, is an inspiration to experience each passing moment as the last; such an attitude gives paramount importance to the actions and thoughts of the here and now, rather than to the past or to the future.

Westerners commonly view the circumstances and belongings of their lives as more or less fixed, or permanent—at least for now. The simple truth of our own impermanence is disguised and diffused by the abundance of possessions with which we surround ourselves. Material possessions help maintain the illusion of permanence and offer some reassurance against our eventual demise. Even those able to acknowledge that death is inevitable are likely to feel that it will not happen for a very long time. Given this attitude of denial, Western thinking around terminal illness and death characteristically focuses on controlling or curing each new physical manifestation of the dying process. Often this is done at the expense of responding to the person as an integrated whole. Narrowly focusing on the disease and avoiding both the subject of dying and the idea of impermanence insures a lack of preparedness that can be devastating when death does strike.

To be alive is to inescapably face death. Knowing that death is imminent can generate fear that is almost unbearable. The ultimate outcome of our lives is always the same and there seems to be nothing we can do about it. Why, then, should we bother thinking about something that we can do nothing about? In the Buddhist view there is good reason to reflect upon our eventual death because something can indeed be done to prepare for and understand it, both intellectually and experientially. This view of life and death is tied to the concept of karma, generally meaning action. In the Buddhist view, every action an individual performs, whether it is positive, negative, or neutral, effects an imprint on his or her mind, and each imprint then becomes a subconscious predisposition towards acting in that same manner again. The Buddha said:

> Mind is the main element and the forerunner of all.
> If with a hateful mind one speaks or acts,
> He suffers because of that,
> Just as the wheel of the cart follows the horse.

The concept that any action undertaken gains strength for its future repetition is not new to Western psychology—we commonly assert that the mind does what it is used to (conditioning), and we often call ourselves "creatures of habit" in the vernacular. Tibetan Buddhists would say that an individual whose actions are altruistic and unselfish tends to create for himself or herself a mind that is predisposed to goodness, whereas an individual whose actions are unkind and malicious tends to create for himself or herself a mind that is predisposed to cruelty.

In the Tibetan Buddhist view our actions and deeds of the past have strongly determined what we are today, and our actions today are greatly influencing the course our life will take in the future. Karma—every action we take, as well as the thought and intention behind that action—becomes the cause of either our happiness or unhappiness. We tend to regard ourselves as passive victims of circumstances, for which we take no responsibility. So the idea that there is no cause for our happiness or unhappiness other than our own actions involves taking full responsibility for ourselves—a potentially discouraging perspective for some people. However, the law of karma can offer encouragement for those willing to take responsibility for their actions, because it affords the opportunity to shape the future with today's action. As the Buddha said, we are our own worst enemy or we are our own savior.

Buddhism teaches the importance of meditating on death every day of one's life. Death meditation is designed to promote a sense of the true meaning and value of a human life. Once one has developed even the smallest awareness of the impermanence of one's life and the unavoidable nature of death, there is an inevitable shift in priorities, and it becomes easier to talk about death and to relate with people who are dying. In Western culture, the lack of exposure to evaluating the meaning of life in terms of death has made it easier for caregivers, patients, and loved ones alike to avoid any psychological interaction with people who are dying. After all, who has time to think about death? Who, having the time, has the inclination? This is especially true in our culture where youth and productivity are so idolized. It is difficult to face the unalterable truth that death will occur for each one of us. And equally difficult to face the unknown world that lies beyond death.

It is troubling to accept that separation from all we hold dear, even our body, is inevitable. Such a thought is psychologically discomforting and undesirable. To accept and understand the dying of another person requires a certain amount of introspection and evaluation regarding the subject of our own death. Most of us do not learn to evaluate our own experiences of loss, death, and impermanence, and thus have not developed a clear and coherent framework by which to explain these events to ourselves. Consequently, denial is the most common reaction when confronted with these issues.

My deepening exposure to Buddhism revealed that reflecting on death and understanding impermanence are not negative, however. Developing an awareness of impermanence can lead to a more expansive mental outlook reaching beyond conventional thinking. Patients, loved ones, and caregivers, struggling with their own fears of death and loss could benefit from the assistance and comfort that an expanded view of death and dying can provide. It has been found, for example, that the people least able to cope with loss and death are those with the greatest need for control, predictability, and security in their world. On the other hand, those who were best able to cope with loss and death were those that could explain the events in terms of an expanded mental outlook. Such an expanded world view allows an individual to acknowledge death, with the uncertainty of its arrival, as a natural and expected part of life, and simultaneously can inspire one to live each moment to the fullest, realizing that nothing is permanent. A recognition of impermanence can catalyze acceptance of the naturalness of dying and death, and an awareness that every moment, whether on the brink of living or dying, has the potential to bring strength and consolation not only to a dying patient but to loved ones and caregivers as well.

I did more emergency nursing in a trauma center in Los Angeles. Gang-related deaths, child abuse deaths, and drug deaths were common and expected daily crises. The psycho-social repercussions of these events would reverberate in the waiting room for hours, while the distraught families waited for some sign from the crews laboring over the body in the trauma room. Everyone desperately hoped that medicine would succeed in gluing the victim back together and thereby avert the necessity of having to face death. If there was no death, they imagined, the nightmare would be over and everything would be all right again.

I started working directly with these anguished families, who were routinely left hoping but helpless in the waiting room, wringing their hands and despairing for information about the prognosis. Just being there physically with them was important. Some of the questions I heard these people asking themselves over and over were: "How can he die?" "Does his death mean that he'll be gone forever?" "If he's gone now then what did his life mean?" "I just saw him a little while ago, how can he possibly be dead?"

Following such a scene the survivors would usually review the victim's life, relating anecdotes about various experiences they remembered about the victim. It was a time of confusion, yet the urgency of the crisis situation also focused and concentrated the participants' thoughts and emotions. They were often eager to discuss ideas regarding the notion that nothing ever really dies, that everything is energy and movement and therefore just endlessly changing. This fundamental recognition of the impermanent nature of life usually manifests when the imminent death of a dear one hovers close by. The situation is so tenuous and the outcome so unpredictable that the usual sense of permanence weakens, opening the door for a deep insight about the impermanent nature of all existence.

Whether as a patient, loved one, or caregiver, the prospect of death usually raises an acute awareness of the myriad changes occurring within the continual passage of time. Watching a disease slowly devour a human body headed toward imminent death is a powerful catalyst for raising questions about material permanence. Deterioration, decay, and the finality of separation from friends, family, pets, money, self-image, prestige, power, and the body is traumatic to imagine, much less to experience. To witness a person taking the last breath and then become absolutely silent and stone-like is an enormous shock to one's usual, naive belief in permanence. Death has an undeniable impact on the human psyche; it is the most existentially profound example of impermanence. For patients, loved ones, and caregivers, being near death and observing impermanence is a shock to certain beliefs about the nature of the self and of the world. We are conditioned to believe that the world is relatively permanent and secure—fixed and unchanging—but being near death dramatically contradicts this view. Facing death, barely conscious beliefs about our immortality lose validity. Facing death can cause feelings of helplessness, of hopelessness, of meaninglessness, and quintessential emotional pain. Yet, this very state of crisis also affords an opportunity to deepen in more positive ways our understanding of death, and more broadly, the changeable, impermanent nature of our conventional, constructed realities.

Realization of this impermanent quality of the human body often gives rise to a recognition of the impermanent quality of all living things and all material things as well. What is born dies and no creature is immortal. The length of one's life is uncertain. To grasp the changeable character of everything further awakens an awareness that not only is each decade, year, month, day, and hour different from the last, but so is each moment. Yet the principle of impermanence and alterability can be applied positively to one's life, thus making personal change possible in any given moment. The very impermanence that we fear also allows for new experiences. When viewed only as the source of death and loss, impermanence is unwelcome. Once seen as the source of all change in our lives, however, we see its positive side. Without impermanence, there would be no maturation, progression, or evolution.

When I worked with a group of men dying of AIDS (Acquired Immune Deficiency Syndrome), we went together through the expected losses, one by one. First the physical losses, then the emotional, and then the intellectual. Invariably this would bring us to the spiritual anguish expressed by most of the terminally ill patients that I have known. Although the clinical process of AIDS varies significantly from patient to patient, sooner or later death makes its appearance. Still it is hard to accept. These men told me of the indescribable terror they felt when they tested positively for the HIV (Human Immuno Virus) antibodies. Because AIDS is such a new disease in our society, denial is the most common reaction. Looking within for internal resources can yield profound insights, yet there is little support for this type of reflection. Buddhism offers much to those facing the anguish of terminal illness.

Buddhism teaches that the recognition of impermanence can lead to transformation, a positive and productive psychological transformation in an individual's basic understanding about himself or herself in relation to the changeable, impermanent nature of the universe. Recognizing the impermanent foundation of the universe—its objects, people, places and ideas, and the constant changes that are taking place within each new moment—provides fertile ground for transformation. The transformation is from the restricted, conventional point of view that fixates upon security and permanence, and consequently a fear of death and change, to an expanded view based on the awareness of the potential for change inherent in all processes. Such an expanded view allows an individual to acknowledge impermanence, death, and the uncertainty of its arrival time as a natural and expected part of life that inspires one to live each precious moment to the fullest. Such a vantage point allows some of the less material wonders of life to be experienced more deeply, such as a bullfrog sitting on glistening, wet grass, illuminated by a round, shining moon—a moon itself always changing. A shift in understanding about priorities in one's life, the inherent meaningfulness of each moment, the very naturalness of dying and death, can offer strength and consolation, and teach us to relish every moment.

Death comes to all. Although modern technology, exemplified in complicated life-support systems, can prolong life in some cases, it still is unable to change the inevitable process of aging and the ultimate finality of certain diseases. Most people continue to cope with the issues of death and dying by avoidance, and the terminally ill are often removed from the population at large. Thus the hospital, instead of the home, has become the usual destination for the terminally ill. Out of sight, they are cared for and eventually die. Watching the body of a person wither away can be frightening, especially for those who feel they must control their lives. The dying process directly and dramatically confronts one with the nature of change inherent in the cycles of existence.

Buddhism was extremely helpful to me during the process of my sister's lingering death two years ago. She was forty-five years old and had very few spiritual aspirations. She was actually fearful and closed to any suggestions that she might find comfort in expanding her degree of awareness and understanding. At first I was extremely upset by her attitude, but then I realized it was not for me to decide what she should or should not do with the last few months of her life. I was with her for support and comfort and not to force her to view her life in a way which was foreign and threatening to her. Enabling a person to accomplish a sense of having lived purposefully and with significance is a major goal of caregivers and loved ones. Being able to support someone during their dying trajectory, regardless of what they are thinking or feeling is probably one of the most valuable services one person can offer to another. But, it is difficult to stay close to someone who is dying. Not trying to evade an open encounter with the intense psychic pain that usually accompanies the recognition of impending death is one of the most valuable contributions that a nurse or any other caregiver or loved one can make to the patient who wishes to discuss his or her circumstances. Facing forthrightly the situation of dying, however, requires feeling comfortable with one's own feelings about death and the frailty of being human.

Buddhism has taught me that death need not be approached only as a tragedy; it is also an event from which a profound understanding can unfold. Caregivers, friends and families should all be encouraged in their work with the dying to deepen their own understanding of death. The sensitivity that we bring to the dying process will certainly shape our interaction with the dying person. We can be most helpful when we understand ourselves. The means to achieve this self-understanding are available—according to Buddhism—by developing insight into the transitory nature of human existence, and expanding our awareness beyond conventional thinking.

Chapter 4
Mothering and Meditation

by Jacqueline Mandell

Sometimes people ask me, "Now that you're a mother, do you still meditate?" That question negates mothering as a meditation. We assume that meditation is only what happens at meditation centers, that we can only be aware on the cushion or in a quiet place. Meditation is not only formal practice. The extraordinary challenge is not only to meditate on the cushion, but to bring complete awareness into our lives. Complete awareness has no sense of separation and no sense of self. It involves no dualism; there is only the undivided moment, the spontaneous present.

It was never my conscious intention to have two young ones. My intention was to have one child, carry it on my back and continue on. Instead, I realized I was going to have twins.

The first two years were very demanding, like the rigorous practice of Rinzai Zen. In fact, nursing one baby and then the other, it was even busier. There wasn't even time to wash up or go to the bathroom in the morning. My children's cries were the gongs and changing diapers was my answer to the *koan*. My husband and I changed twelve thousand diapers, like beads of a *mala*.

The first week my children were home, a friend drove down and said, "I am here to serve you." She stayed for a week—cooking, cleaning, and looking after the children when I took a walk.

This is called "mother care" and I would like to introduce it to our list of social services. Buddhists are doing so many wonderful things: for peace, death and dying, AIDS, ecology. But are Buddhists serving women? Is anyone helping mothers? Is anyone doing childcare? Our services could be even more wonderful.

In the context of scriptural Buddhism, with its focus on monastic practice, the choice to become a mother is a significant statement. For me, being a mother has been very nourishing. There is a tremendous dynamic that takes place between mother and child. When my children were first born, I knew, of course, that they were already spiritual, already intelligent, already healthy. All I need to give them is love and honesty. That is my primary goal in parenting.

Sometimes it has been frustrating, just being at home, feeling hopeless. I'd think, "What am I doing? Society doesn't pay us, doesn't value us." Yet to learn from a child is an honor. As we cultivate loving-kindness with children, the whole give and take is our practice.

Some friends and I decided to create a mothers' meditation group. Our commitment was to meditate with our children. It took us a few times to get it together, and each time we met, it was different. At first we tried to go to another room, but the children would cry, so we realized that wouldn't work and made the adjustment. Sometimes it was a bit complex with only two mothers: one baby would be playing, and I would be meditating with the other one on my lap. One day one of my daughters lined up all her stuffed animals and they were all meditating!

I also teach my children non-harm, non-hate, and non-delusion. I taught them loving-kindness before they began to speak. We live in an area where there are centipedes, scorpions, tarantulas, black widow spiders, and sometimes snakes. When we see insects, we put them in a cup and carry them outside. When we see a bee or a fly, we also help it to find its way out. Whenever the children see an insect, they call me to bring my cup and transport it to another location. They really love insects and have learned to identify them. I found a picture of a centipede in a book called *To Be Alive* and told the girls if they saw one, not to touch it, but to call me. They have learned non-harm this way, by example. They never harm living creatures; it would never enter their minds.

I have also taught them non-greed. In a toy store, we play with the toys, put them back, and say good-bye. They have not learned that people need to *buy* the things in the stores. When we talk about shopping, it is for food. I teach them to make choices without grasping at things, and to make intelligent choices without fear.

Before becoming a mother, I taught meditation for a number of years. I remembered that a teacher of mine, Dipa Ma, lived in one room in Calcutta and taught at home. So one day I thought, "That's it. I'll teach at home." My husband takes the children out and I turn our front room into a meditation space with an incense ceremony. People really like to meditate in this spacious environment, and I don't have to separate myself from my home and children.

Sometimes people ask how I balance non-attachment and mothering. All my training has been in developing non-attachment and the birth of my children has also been a process of developing non-attachment. Just before they turned two, I began using a babysitter while I taught two meditation classes a week. Fortunately, I found a warm, loving, responsive grandmother, who cares for them with great kindness. The children experienced being part of another household, like children in other countries who are naturally cared for by grandmothers, aunts, and uncles from the start. Each month I would leave my children for awhile and last year, for the first time, I was away at a Dzogchen retreat for four nights. The whole process was very organic.

I was hesitant at first to leave them, but some friends encouraged me to resume teaching after I became a mother. It was very healthy for them to have another source of nourishment at that time, since I was weaning them. I have found that children have their own karma. We can't always lead them around and create ideal circumstances for them. There are karmic forces at work and decisions to be made based on those karmic conditions.

Sometimes I take them to see Tibetan lamas, and they spend the day where I am teaching. They recognize the Buddha and ask if they can eat the bananas, apples, and other offerings on the altar. They have their own perceptions and associations. Whenever they see a Buddha, they fold their hands in prayer.

When I was teaching and leading long retreats at meditation centers, I was always available to answer questions. But I began to wonder if it is healthy for someone to always be available. If children feel secure and their self-esteem is sufficient, both sides can begin letting go. For the first ten months, my children slept with me in the family bed. I was there for them when they wanted to nurse and their needs were met. Now my children understand when I go away and just wave good-bye at the airport.

Of course, people have different styles of parenting. Some can stay home and some cannot. Some can find really qualified childcare and some cannot. I have found that much of parenting is creating self-esteem and reassuring children so they don't spend the rest of their lives trying to meet their childhood needs. There's a wonderful saying: "Children can't leave home until they've been home."

In the Dzogchen practice that I am doing now, there is childcare on every retreat. The first time I took my children to a retreat, I was hesitant. It was really a surprise to find that people were happy that my children came! It worked out beautifully. When I went to the meditation room, they ran around the yard. During the chanting, visualization, and drumming that goes with Chö practice, one of my daughters lay in my lap. When the chanting ended, she started clapping and you could tell that she was quite energized by the practice. My wonderful, supportive husband was in charge of childcare at that retreat.

Since motherhood, I have had to re-examine almost every particle of my Buddhist practice. The main shift has been to emphasize relaxed awareness—relaxed, yet precise awareness. My entire Buddhist training was in awareness and mindfulness, based on calm concentration. Concentration feels wonderful, but it is also impermanent. People get attached to that wonderful feeling and become disappointed when they can't carry it into their daily lives. Now I teach students just to relax into each moment, rather than pushing through, and this makes the transition easier. Usually after retreats, where we eat and sleep less, people suddenly grasp at sweets and food. They act like they have been in prison, instead of retreat. But recently, after teaching relaxed awareness at a retreat at Lama Foundation, people ate moderately and spoke quietly. The cooks were astounded.

Our socio-economic system in the West produces many tensions in people's lives. Our lives are a kind of rushing forward, and there is even a lot of effort in the retreats we do. Most of my training was very austere—an effortful, breakneck approach. I had a teacher who had not lain down in thirty-eight years! In contrast, Dzogchen practice emphasizes relaxation and calm awareness, along with concentration.

I also began using the Buddhist teachings on dependent origination and the twelve links of causation. I taught awareness at the moment of contact: awareness of seeing, hearing, smelling, tasting, and touching. By not following desire, aversion, attachment, or delusion, this awareness cuts through defilements. In the middle of the retreat, somebody asked for the umpteenth time, "How do you take this into daily life?" This reminded me of the teaching on the twelve links. After contact comes feeling. If the feeling is pleasurable, it leads to desire. If the feeling is neutral, it leads to spacing out, not knowing, or ignorance. If the feeling is painful, it leads to aversion, aversion leads to hatred, and hatred leads to actions we will regret. Trying for the pleasant and pushing away the unpleasant only creates dualism and suffering.

Another thing I learned was that people at retreats want to be outdoors, where it is so beautiful. I used to think that seeing pleasant things led to attachment, but I've found that there is a way of noticing pleasant things without cultivating greed and attachment. I've found that I can notice a beautiful tree while doing walking meditation. I can stop to notice a tree, notice that the tree is beautiful, and just be aware of the pleasantness of the present moment. Feelings are part of meditation, and are not necessarily bad.

The Dharma needs to be adaptable and inclusive. If it is only for monasteries, childless women, women with grown children, women who can afford child care, or women with supportive husbands, we are in trouble. We have a fringe religion. No matter how many women have become enlightened before us, no matter how many enlightened women are mentioned in the scriptures, no matter how many enlightened women are revered, unless it translates into society, it is useless.

Recently I had a dream that was a very clear and spontaneous message. The dream was of the first woman, standing very elegantly and looking at an egg before her. Sequence by sequence, she saw all the destruction that could befall the egg. It could be crushed, eaten, blown away, or damaged in so many different ways. And the first woman, out of compassion for the suffering of the egg, lifted it up and put it inside of her body, so that the wisdom of the ages could be safely carried through. This dream was in total contrast to the popular Buddhist conception that a woman is a lesser birth: that she takes a lower birth due to bad karma created in a past life, gives birth, and thus suffers more. The dream was of the woman and mother as a bodhisattva, a caring and compassionate one, a preserver of life, actively transforming wisdom and life itself.

After this dream, any remnants of dualistic attitudes I had about women completely fell away. When I see other women, when I see mothers, my respect for them is so deep. Now my respect for the entire lay community is far richer and far deeper than it ever was before.

When I lived in monasteries, I felt superior. When lay people asked questions about their lives, I was giving answers about something that was not in my experience. The monastic system is a great gift for the preservation of Buddhism and this should never be forgotten. But it also involves hierarchy, with the male monk at the top, and laypeople and mothers hovering somewhere on the bottom. Through sharing my experiences of having been both a mother and a monastic, I try to dispel this dualist conception.

There are many issues to consider concerning mothering and meditation. Pregnant women may feel a division in their own identity between meditating and mothering. Sometimes meditation practice can become intense and stir things up, which may be a problem during pregnancy. Meditation has different aspects: concentration, effort, as well as deep calm. It would seem valuable to practice the calming aspect of meditation during pregnancy. Stress can adversely affect the life force and serenity of the child, while if the mother practices the calming aspect, the child will become habituated to a sense of calm. When a woman is pregnant, nurturing another being, she is in a very open psychic space, susceptible to all sorts of influences, whether conscious or unconscious. So it is important that the environment around her be full of loving-kindness, without prejudice, fear, or negativity. Practice should not be given up during pregnancy, but it should be approached with caution. And there are certain practices that pregnant women are advised not to undertake.

Another problem is: Who cares for the mothers with small children? The United States and South Africa are among the only countries in the world with no mother care. Just as we care immeasurably for mother earth, because she is willing to give, we need to support the mothers who give us children. We need to develop an attitude of helping these women. Just to walk into a new mother's house and sweep her floor is a wonderful offering. Mothers are expected to nourish, but mothers need nourishing, too. In this way, Buddhist women can be of great service.

A strong foundation of meditation practice beforehand helps handle the demands of parenting. I could mother intensively because of the years and years of intensive practice I did in Burma, Thailand, India, and Mt. Baldy. Many mothers cannot deal with the stress, especially in cases of substance abuse, as in Chicago where thirty-five percent of the babies are born addicted.

Images projected onto women have their effect. There are wonderful role models in Buddhism of women who have been mothers and teachers. There is the bodhisattva practice of generating respect for our mothers in past incarnations, but there are other less positive forms of conditioning in both Eastern and Western religions. Woman as temptress becomes a singular image. We need to recognize these projected images, identify and discuss them, in order to be liberated from them. For example, in India, although mothers are deified, women are not. This is a problem. Even the words used to describe women are important. For example, if the word for "woman" means "lesser birth" and this word has been used for thousands of years, it has an effect on people. We need to dispel the myth that being a woman is a lower birth, not only on a societal level, but also on levels that we have unconsciously internalized. Attitudes which degrade the important task of mothering also harm children by association. Such attitudes reflect a lack of experience and understanding about the nature of children.

We tend to share certain pervasive social assumptions or ideas about gender. It is as if the cards have been dealt out and women got the ones saying "body," "childbirth," "feelings," "nature," and so on. Certain qualities become associated with women, although they don't always fit. When we project these stereotypes onto women, the belief system becomes perpetuated. If the traits associated with women are negative or demeaning, all women become degraded.

With a compassionate attitude of wishing to prevent harm, we need to isolate all aspects of the problems women face in spiritual practice, discussing them with an attitude of becoming liberated from these problems. We need to face the problems people have with honoring women and childbirth. Rather than thinking of life and giving life as a curse because it inevitably entails suffering and death, we can see life as an opportunity for reaching enlightenment. In this way, we can pass on to our children a less dualistic approach.

There are many intelligent, educated women and men practicing Buddhism now. It is a tremendous opportunity and responsibility to re-examine the tradition and effect profound changes, a time of boundless potential and possibility. We need to look at the whole system, assessing the teachings and taking the true essence, not just meditate. We need to incorporate the authentic and valuable elements of the belief system and abandon those elements that only create more dualistic thinking. That's how Buddhism will be modified by our culture. We don't devalue or criticize it—that's just the same old pattern of delusion in our mind—but what we uphold will be what carries forward.

Furyu: Previously, I was very intent on monastic experience. When I went to Tassajara Monastery, they were experimenting with involving children. Those of us who were without children were rather horrified by this prospect. At a special ceremony, when each of us was given a task, I was assigned to the baths. This was a great blessing, because I could be alone in the bathhouse all day. Then a woman was asked to do childcare, but having just raised twin boys, she refused the task. This was unheard of—no one had ever refused a task before.

So I was given the assignment of looking after the children all day: a one-year-old, a two-year-old, and a three-year-old. In the beginning we all just stared at each other, but in the end they completely captured me. At the work meetings, they would jump out of their parents' arms and run to me. It was wonderful. Now these children are teenagers and off to college.

After helping the children as they grow up, the next phase is helping them as they look for something deeper in their lives. It is lucky we have something to offer them.

Response: Thich Nhat Hanh, who brought me to Buddhism, does a lot of work with children. At a retreat with him, I had the privilege of taking part in the care of small children, which was one of the most valuable parts of the retreat for me. I had an opportunity to speak with parents about meditating with children. Usually it is the mothers themselves who forfeit going to the Dharma talk to care for the children. It is really important for others to become aware and involved in the care of children at retreats.

Response: As a mother of grown children, I would like to explore the problem of attachment a little further. In Marpa's biography, it tells that when his son died he was crying. His student asked him why he was crying, since it's all an illusion, and he said, "It's a very sad illusion."

Jacqueline: Non-attachment does not mean non-experience or stoicism. We want to be able to face life in a forceful way. Non-attachment does not mean appearances or denial, like bearing up at funerals with a stiff upper lip. Non-attachment means understanding that the natural process of our experience is impermanent: arising, abiding, and passing away. Non-attachment means not grasping at feelings. With children, this means not being elated when they are good or disappointed when they misbehave. It doesn't mean pushing the children away. Mothering, for me, means being undividedly with my children, fully in the present, rather than wanting to change or manipulate them. This allows for a natural letting go. It's not: "I'm compassionate because I'm a Buddhist and I'm raising my children to be Buddhists." It's not some package deal like that.

Response: One of the few times I have been in the moment was when my son was born. I had been told all through the pregnancy that he was probably going to be born a vegetable. My husband at that time had tremendous faith and chanted the "Om Mani Padme Hum" mantra every night. I was trying to reject the spiritual path at the time and saw this as a kind of denial. After a ten-month pregnancy, my son was born and it was a very difficult labor. When he came out, he weighed only five pounds and was blue, like Krishna. He looked dead. In that moment, I realized fully that he might only live for ten minutes, so I had to transcend my attachment. I had to create a peaceful space for him in that moment, facing death. I experienced our interconnectedness and projected nothing onto him. It was not a matter of not crying or not feeling, but of viewing things dispassionately. Non-attachment allows us to *really* experience the moment and to touch a greater truth.

Response: What is our obligation as receivers of the teachings? Do we accept everything written in the texts or are there levels of spiritual growth, moments of revelation, that go beyond the texts?

Jacqueline: We need to remember that cultural values inform religious traditions and teachers, even Buddha. We need to be true to our cultural values as well. But the devaluation of women and mothering are not simply carryovers from ancient cultures. Indifference and cruelty to women and children are endemic in American culture, too. In some cultures, it is women who perpetuate cruelty upon other women, for example, with clitoridectomy. Life is not perfect anywhere in the world and we make a mistake if we unrealistically attribute ideal conditions to other cultures. They all have their shadow side. When the Buddha taught the First Noble Truth, that there is suffering, he was referring to everyone.

Eko Susan: The perspective of Buddhism is not a singular model or exclusive way, but a path leading to greater understanding, compassion, and wisdom. Although we may undergo periods of strict training, the goal is not to sit on top of a mountain for the rest of our lives. Our work is in the world. The aspiration to help others is the most precious gift we can give.

We should never underestimate the profound changes that are possible through training the body and mind. Strict celibacy is maintained during intensive practice periods, because the practices effect powerful changes. The reason why women should not be pregnant when they do certain kinds of training, especially tantra, is that the changes in the body might occur too fast to accommodate the new life that is there. The primary reason for maintaining celibacy is to preserve the various energies of the body. Other traditions of meditation are less taxing. For example, one woman had no problem doing Zen training at Tassajara while pregnant with twins. All these different experiences, every piece of information, is important, because pregnant women are coming to retreats and we do not have enough knowledge to address that. We need to read the texts, talk to teachers, and find out all we can.

Tsering: In the Mahayana tradition, motherhood is highly venerated. Giving life to a human being is an exalted action. The pain of it is not considered degrading. Instead, to bear the pain to allow another being to have a precious human birth and the chance to attain enlightenment is considered virtuous. When Chakdud Rinpoche's grandson was born, the mother went into retreat. Rinpoche told her, "There is no greater retreat you can do than to raise that child." She and her husband did retreats with the baby. She does her practice and she raises her child. To bring up a child in a Dharma environment, with Buddhist principles from early on, is a highly respected approach to practice.

Response: Yvonne Rand used to ask, "If raising children is such a venerated practice, why aren't monks encouraged to do it?"

Tsering: Many do. Chakdud Rinpoche was raised under the constant care of a monk. Young children were raised by monks in many monasteries. Sometimes the teachings I receive from my child are more valuable than anything I get when I go away on retreat. I try to remind myself that my child's learning, unfolding, and awakening also awaken me. I want my whole life to be my practice. Things change as the child grows up. My son has an orbit pattern. He orbits, and he always comes back, but his orbit gets bigger year by year. We train in doing everyday practice; if we can't meditate when a child is crying, how will we meditate when we're dying? As we mature in our practice, we gradually stop attempting to separate meditation and real life. Eventually, we find that there is no difference between the two. No one is excluded from our shrine room, including the animals.

Eko Susan: Children intuitively understand Dharma, without making value judgments about it. They just watch. In the Shingon tradition, we use form, sound, and everything to teach. Once in Vermont, a teacher set up a small altar with all the ritual implements and was very busy going through all the rituals, making mudras, and performing different blessings. Before him, sitting with her mother, was a very precocious four-year-old girl, watching and taking it all in. After the ceremony finished, we took a break and went to eat in the other room. All of a sudden, we heard a little voice chanting. When we looked in the room, the little girl had sat herself behind the altar and was making her own mudras, chanting her own mantras, and giving blessings with the stick. It was clear that this child had an intuitive sense of it all, so we asked her to teach us. We sat there as her students, and she was as happy as a clam. There are great lessons we can learn from children.

Michelle: I had been going to retreats for about twelve years and had never seen a child at one. The retreats were conducted in the monastic style, in complete silence. Just a few years ago, interested in experiencing his teaching style, I went to my first retreat with Thich Nhat Hanh. But when I arrived, I was amazed and shocked to see many children running around! I thought, "Oh, no! What is this? How are we going to meditate?" But Thich Nhat Hanh didn't treat the children as distractions at all. They were the most important people there. They sat in the front row and could sit as long as they wanted to. The first fifteen minutes of the Dharma talk was also for them—the quintessence of Buddhism that even a child could understand.

Then in the afternoon, we had tea ceremony, with the children as tea ceremony masters. Instead of just being spectators, they were greeting people at the door, showing them to their seats, and passing out cookies and tangerines. There was also an afternoon sharing with the children, where we sang songs, shared poems, told stories, or expressed insights. The questions they asked totally shattered my preconceptions about children. My admiration for them skyrocketed during the retreat. We learned to see the wisdom in their eyes.

Another interesting experience I had was talking with Maria, the mother of the child who has been recognized as the incarnation of Lama Yeshe, a wonderful Tibetan teacher who passed away in 1984. Lama Yeshe was reborn as a Spanish boy to a couple of his students who had a retreat center in Grenada. I remember when I met Lama Yeshe in his new form as a twenty-month-old baby. Even though Maria was a Buddhist, she came from a Catholic background and would not use birth control. When she already had four children, she asked Lama Yeshe for a blessing so she wouldn't have more children, but Lama said, "Oh, but you'd make such a good mother." She was so sad to say goodbye to him, but he looked at her very deeply and said, "Don't be sad that I'm leaving. We'll be doing a very long retreat together."

Jacqueline: We need to have our arms wide open to embrace all the differences in how we decide to practice, as women, as human beings, from different backgrounds, traditions, and experiences. We need to choose the ground that is most fertile for us. For some, monastic situations provide the atmosphere to produce wonderful things. For others, the path is producing children and bringing life into being. We need to be very flexible, balanced, and harmonious concerning ways of being in this universe. In a spirit of openness and inclusiveness, we can dispel all the ordinary value judgments that constantly propel the wheel of samsara. We become empowered by our diversity.

When a Buddhist woman has a baby, the perceptive question is not: "Now that you're a mother, do you still meditate?" A kinder question would be, "Now that you're a mother, may I help you so that you can meditate?"

Chapter 5
Everyday Dharma

by Michelle Levey

How do we integrate our spiritual practice into our daily life and professional work? How do we really bring it alive in the world, make it acceptable to our friends, co-workers, and clients? How do we celebrate our interconnectedness in our work and in our relationships in the world?

I became a Buddhist practitioner in 1975 and took my first Vipassana course with Ruth Dennison in British Columbia, overcoming my intellectual resistance to organized religion. For me, Buddhism was like coming home. I remember taking refuge, taking refuge in the truth, and slowly beginning to see what was really meant by those words. A whole transformation occurred then and life has never really been the same since. As I reflect upon it, it was fitting that a woman teacher introduced me to Buddhism. Vipassana ("insight") meditation was my main practice for about seven years. I also spent some time at a Zen monastery in Japan. Later I was introduced in an intimate, direct way to the Tibetan teachings.

In 1982, Geshe Ngawang Dhargyey came to Seattle and taught Tibetan iconography at the University of Washington, demystifying mandalas and explaining all the symbolism. In the Philosophy

Department he taught the philosophy of the Middle Way, or Madhyamika. After classes and on weekends, too, we continued these conversations as we walked home with him. It was an intensive plunge.

My practice had been going along steadily, and yet there was something missing. I had not quite known what it was, but I found it in Geshe Dhargyey's teachings. I began integrating the foundational practice of vipassana meditation with the Mahayana aspiration. I feel very blessed to have studied and developed special connections with wonderful teachers from all four schools of the Tibetan tradition. I also had the good fortune to attend retreats with Thich Nhat Hanh, a very special bodhisattva and great teacher of our times.

In the world I work as a bio-feedback therapist, doing psychophysical training in private practice. This becomes a door into meditation for many people. Recognizing that the mind is connected with the body, they come to work with me to investigate this connection, and discover an interest in meditation.

I do about ninety percent of my work in tandem with my husband and co-facilitate a weekly meditation course with him at our home on Tuesday nights. We do a lot of corporate consulting, workshops with health-care and other professionals, and work with both teachers and students in mental fitness training and stress mastering.

For many people the search for mental development begins with health problems. They want to learn some skills for dealing with the stresses of daily life. Gradually they develop an understanding of the human mind and its potential. We always try to keep the motivation and the scope as great as possible, so that people can just grow into a larger field of awareness.

My peace activist work began in 1985 when I was part of a six-month training program for the Special Forces—the Green Berets. My husband and I took a group of twenty for a one-month meditation retreat in New Hampshire. It was a wonderful opportunity and also quite a challenge to meet face-to-face all our prejudices about the military. Together with our students, we began to let go of our cultural conditioning and see things from other perspectives. We dropped our prejudgments and accepted others simply as human beings, all in samsara together, all wanting to be happy.

Then in 1988, I had the good fortune to do a one-year silent shamata ("calm abiding") retreat in the Tibetan tradition, focusing on developing strong one-pointed concentration. Shamata meditation is common to all the different traditions of Buddhism and is practiced in certain non-Buddhist traditions as well. The practice helps develop the power of the mind to stay focused. Once this one-pointed concentration is developed, we can then proceed to vipassana meditation, tantra, and other practices.

My motivation for doing the retreat was to develop some skills that I could share with other people so I could really be of service in the world. After the retreat, we had many requests from mainstream organizations to lead programs and workshops. The universe is responsive, and in ever-expanding ways I have been working closely with corporate change, helping people who are looking for deep and lasting ways to transform organizations. These groups have various motivations, of course, but some are spiritually inclined. We try to create an awareness that to make changes in organizations, one needs to develop the mind and pay attention to what is going on inside. Beginning on the psycho-physical level, learning to observe motivations, thoughts, and emotions, we try to bring meditation into the mainstream.

How do we fashion our daily lives so that we contribute to the spiritual growth of ourselves and others, so that there is no separation between our meditation practice and our relationships and our work in the world? Here I would like to share with you a sequence of meditations that I have found useful in my own life. Each of these meditations is complete in itself and each ties into the theme of human interaction and the interrelatedness of all life. All are based on the understanding that we are not alone; we live in relationship with others. Our meditation practice is intimately connected to other people—in our work and in every aspect of our lives.

We begin with a short prayer and meditation on going for refuge to the Three Jewels (Buddha, Dharma, and Sangha) and generating the altruistic aspiration to attain enlightenment. This is a way of remembering our connectedness both vertically to the sources of inspiration and blessing in our lives and horizontally to the whole community and the world.

Let your eyes close softly or let them be softly open, whichever is more comfortable. Imagine yourself sitting in the center of a mandala of your friends and relations. Visualize in the space in front of you a cloud of all the sources of joy and inspiration in your life—teachers who show the way, spiritual books, the Buddha, the Dharma, the exalted Sangha, and the bodhisattvas of all times. Visualizing these objects of refuge before us, we also take refuge in our inner teacher. Imagine this noble assembly looking upon us with much love and affection, and feel a sense of personal connection with all these sources of blessing and inspiration.

On your left, imagine all the women in your life, beginning with your mother, sisters, relatives, friends, and all female sentient beings extending infinitely. On your right, imagine all the men in your life: your father, your brothers, relatives, friends, and all the male beings in the world, extending out and filling space. Behind you, imagine all the friends who have given you support, encouraged you in your spiritual development and your life in general: all benefactors, kind friends, and helpers. In the space in front of you, imagine all those beings with whom you have had difficult relations, where there is unfinished business or healing work to be done. Extend the circle out on all sides until space is filled with all living beings in all worlds. We are related to all these sentient beings.

Feel yourself receiving the blessings and inspiration of the enlightened ones—of the Three Jewels and all realized beings. These blessings are the life force that nourishes our practice. To the degree that our hearts are open and receptive to these waves of blessings, we are able to experience inspiration and strength.

Maintaining the sense of connectedness to all living beings, say this prayer three times:

> I and all sentient beings until we attain enlightenment
> Go for refuge to the Buddha, Dharma, and Sangha.
> Through the virtues I collect by giving and other perfections,
> May I become a Buddha for the benefit of all.

As we say this prayer, we imagine leading all sentient beings toward Buddhahood. At the same time, we radiate light to fill the universe, that others may receive blessing and inspiration in the same way.

Then we move into a circle for a meditation adopted from the Native American tradition which is really Buddhist in spirit. Understanding and appreciating our interconnectedness with all of life, we join hands, keeping the awareness of our interrelatedness. We hold hands and join together as one heart, verbally passing around the circle the phrase "all my relations." We evoke an awareness of our connectedness, an appreciation of the vast circle of relationships, as large as the mind can imagine. We include all living beings in all dimensions of existence. As we say "all my relations," we give a little squeeze to the hand of the person on our left, sending an impulse of energy around the circle.

Doing this with just women together is a real treat. Let the words flow swiftly like a river, without any break or hesitation. Your eyes can be gently closed or softly open, but stay centered. Be aware of your breath, your body, the sound of the voices as they travel around the circle, and the flow of the energy created.

The message is that I and all my relations join together as one heart, one mind, to give thanks. This is an honoring of our interdependence and our interconnectedness on all levels. Just allow spontaneous imagery to arise—of people you know, people in the Middle East, suffering beings, joyful beings, world leaders. Be really open and extend your awareness of our interconnectedness to all.

As we open our eyes, we maintain a sense of connection with others. We dispel any fear of vulnerability, any sense of judgment that may arise. What do we notice happening in our body as this sharing begins? Is it easy or difficult to maintain the awareness of arms, breath, sound, and connectedness?

Response: How do we know if we're really in the moment?

Michelle: The awareness that is in the moment and simply notices has a quality of honesty and authenticity. You will know it. We feel a wonderful spiritual connection with everyone during this meditation, but may feel a bit scared when we open our eyes. Some people feel apprehensive afterwards when they begin to interact, feeling they may lose that spiritual connection. Many people, women in particular, feel apprehensive because they feel they are constantly nourishing others, but not receiving nourishment themselves. This meditation helps create a feeling of balance in giving and receiving.

Response: The atmosphere here is rarefied, a very elegant state of being, so it is easy to connect with people with lots of love. The experience could become addictive. It is easy enough to feel only good things while we are in this special atmosphere, but when we go out in the world, we experience a lot of anger and negativity in our daily life, at work, and so on. It is hard to stay positive.

Michelle: The joy we feel at special times in a meditative environment strengthens our capacity to handle all these difficulties, to keep "surfing the waves." Meditation helps us cultivate a positive strength of mind, especially in the midst of darkness. When we find ourselves in difficult situations, these sources of inspiration sustain us. We often get caught up in what's not right in our lives and in our relationships, and don't spend equal time considering what's not wrong. Our attitudes are very unbalanced.

Response: They say that the energy field of plants can be measured, and if there is a threat or danger in the room, houseplants sense it and shut down immediately. I feel like that—that I am shut down most of the time.

Michelle: Humans also have the power to generate energy fields around themselves. It may be one of, say, fear: What is going to happen when I enter a relationship? In actuality, we can determine what we hold in our mind and hearts. We don't have to be bombarded. The thoughts and intentions we generate also cause ripples, creating effects. We live in a two-way world, open on both sides. We may receive what other people are creating, but we are also empowered and have the capacity to concentrate, to will, to imagine, to create, and to generate the type of field that we want to bring into the world. We can create an experience of openness and warmth and love.

For instance, when Gen Lamrimpa, the Tibetan lama who led our one-year retreat, was in Seattle in 1988, he told us a wonderful story. He escaped from Communist-controlled Tibet and had been in retreat in Dharamsala for 15 years. When a group of us expressed a desire to do this retreat, we requested His Holiness the Dalai Lama to send someone to guide us. His Holiness asked Gen Lamrimpa to lead this retreat. His answer was: "Whatever will be of the greatest benefit to the Dharma and sentient beings, I will do."

Gen Lamrimpa had never seen an airplane, so when he went to New Delhi and boarded a plane for the first time, he was truly amazed, like a child. He said it was like being in a new world, taking a new life. He got really worried when he saw all the people and all the baggage being loaded onto the plane. He thought the plane would be too heavy to lift off the ground.

Here was someone with a highly developed inner technology seeing material technology for the first time. All the energy and attention that our culture has put into creating airplanes and material things, Tibetan culture has put into investigating the mind and developing states of awareness. This contrast is really striking.

When we went to welcome Gen Lamrimpa and thank him for coming, it was garbage collection day and there was a lot of noise on the street. He wondered what this banging was all about, so I explained that in this country people come around and pick up your garbage. And he said, "How very kind of them!" His comment changed my whole perspective.

As we were preparing for the retreat, we realized that there were many obstacles that could prevent us from doing it, such as health, parents' health, lack of money, and so on. So we asked him for advice, magic mantras, or some kind of protection that would prevent hindrances. Right away he used an appropriate metaphor. He said, "As you are driving down the freeway in your car, recognize that all the people on the freeway want to reach their destination—some place that will bring them happiness and fulfillment. Just radiate to them: May you reach your destination safely. Cultivating that attitude will be the best protection you can have." I remember asking, "But what if they don't have a positive goal in mind?" and he said, "That's none of your business. You are cultivating your mind wishing for their happiness. Do not concern yourself with judging the correctness of their goal."

Creating a field of loving kindness like this is a very powerful meditation for daily life. Loving kindness and a good heart create the most powerful protection. The red cord that lamas give as a blessing during ceremonies actually stands for loving kindness. Buddha Shakyamuni was able to overcome all hindrances and temptations through the power of his loving kindness.

I learned a very beneficial technique for generating loving kindness and transforming negativity from a Bengali teacher of the Burmese Theravada tradition, Dipa Ma. She is considered a saint, highly attained, and pure of mind. When someone asked her, "What are the qualities of your mind?" she answered, "My mind has three qualities: concentration, equanimity, and loving kindness. That's it."

In this meditation, we focus awareness on the flow of the breath rising and falling in the chest. Notice any feelings of warmth, tingling, vibration, or movement at the heart and allow that region to become soft, open, and radiant. All of us can remember being in the presence of someone with strong loving kindness. Bask in that feeling of warmth, affection, and caring.

To do this meditation authentically, first we need to send a lot of love to ourselves. This is very difficult for some people, but to perfect this practice, we need to care about ourselves, too. We bring to mind our own image, like looking in a mirror, and repeat the following phrases softly:

> *May I be free from enmity:* May I be free from aversion, ill will, hatred, and anger, hostility, and irritation toward myself and others.
> *May I be free from danger:* May I be free from all harms, diseases, accidents, and other dangers.
> *May I be free from disease:* May I be healthy on all levels.
> *May I be happy:* May my heart be open, truly happy, and all wishes fulfilled.
> *May I be free from suffering:* May I be free from all physical, mental, and emotional sufferings.

As we breathe in, we breathe in all feelings of loving kindness, happiness, and caring, filling our whole being.

Next, calling to mind an image of a teacher or friend who has been very kind, visualize someone who naturally arouses these feelings. Focus on that person as representing all our kind relatives, friends, benefactors, and helpers. Behold that person's face as clearly and vividly as possible, generate loving kindness, and again repeat:

> *May you be free from enmity.*
> *May you be free from danger.*
> *May you be free from disease.*
> *May you be happy.*
> *May you be free from suffering.*

Now allow that image to dissolve back into empty space and out of that emptiness, generate an awareness of all the suffering beings in the world, a general, pervasive sense of all the many beings around the globe who are suffering mentally, physically, and emotionally. Allow the spontaneous flow of images to arise in your mind, direct the focus of your concentration on loving kindness to all types of suffering beings, and repeat:

> *May we be free from enmity.*
> *May we be free from disease.*
> *May we be free from danger.*
> *May we be happy.*
> *May we be free from suffering.*

Imagine what it would be like to go beyond the words of this meditation to the feelings pointed to by the words. Imagine what it would be like to build the strength of those feelings so that they become a radiant powerful way of being with which to move through our daily life and work. Our life can become a source of blessing to the world or it can add to the already mounting confusion and anxiety. The choice is up to us. Through "everyday Dharma" practice, we begin building the foundation of right relations. This allows our minds to be calm and free from turbulence. A calm mind, in turn, is the necessary foundation for developing concentration and clarity, which allow the emergence of wisdom and insight. Through deepening insight, our compassion also deepens and manifests as even better relations in our day-to-day life. In this way, our practice follows the cycle of the three higher trainings of ethics, concentration, and wisdom. We go full-circle in an ever-increasing upward spiral of integrating and celebrating the inextricable interweaving of our spiritual work and our daily lives.

Chapter 6
Bringing Dharma into Relationships

by Karuna Dharma

I would like to share a few things I have learned over the years about bringing Dharma into relationships. Human relations is the area in which our practice is most seriously tested. By looking at our relationships, we can gauge the progress of our practice and see how profoundly it is affecting our lives.

In a room with forty people, there are forty different universes. Each one of us sits at the center of our universe. Because it is a universe that we have created, we believe in it. The problem is that each of us views our individual universe from our own particular little time and space, and our universes do not always coincide, so frictions develop. Each of us sits and looks at the others, honestly not understanding what has created the disharmony. Each of us creates our own fictitious universe which we genuinely believe to be true. This can cause serious problems when we become involved in relationships.

How do we solve these problems? How do we remove the barrier that we have drawn around our little universe so we won't be constantly bumping and grating against someone else's? The best way is to drop all the defenses we've thrown up to protect the person who sits in the middle of that universe. We spend so much time building and shoring up these defenses. That means less time is spent in communicating directly.

Where do the defenses come from? Our defenses are there to protect the fictitious universe we have fabricated and regard as true. I may not buy your fabrication, because I didn't create it, but I buy mine and I know mine is superior to yours. See? This is what really interferes with our human relationships. We very busily try to keep a fiction going that is all of our own creation.

Suppose we are on a train and see, for just one second, something happening outside the window. How accurate is our interpretation of that event? How much can we understand of the image we see? We peek into each other's universes for a brief moment, as if passing on a speeding train, yet we're very quick to interpret what we glimpsed in that moment. We are sure our interpretation is correct. This is very dangerous.

If I can free myself from what I have fabricated, there will be no need to continue building or repairing my defenses. And the fewer defenses I have, the better I can communicate and understand you, because I no longer feel threatened. What you think of me means nothing if I feel secure. I only feel fearful because my view of reality has been threatened. The problem is not that someone has been talking behind my back; the problem is that I found out about it and I don't deserve it.

We can disagree about things, but why should that cause conflict? We may never agree on some things, because we perceive things from different angles, but that doesn't have to result in conflict. Why should we be upset because we disagree? When we don't have anything to protect, there is no longer anything to fear. We can experience everything fully, which is wonderful. We can really enjoy being in other people's company, because we're not busy maintaining our own identity. Why waste the time? Why create the anger and the hurt?

We need to let go, but it is not easy. The closer the relationship, the closer we come to our image of who we are. The closer things strike this concept of self we have fabricated, the more difficult it is. Meditation can be very helpful here. We need just be aware and observe without making any judgments, without adding any filters or interpretations. We just hear the sounds, observe the view, and become one with all of it, without feeling any separation. This can help us change our viewpoint and interpretation of the self. We don't have to protect ourselves from the little bird that just went by; we just hear it.

We can begin knocking down the barriers in everything we do— in groups, at work, with our friends, our boss, our lover. If something disturbs us, we can just observe it, and gradually we become a bit more objective. When someone says something, we don't automatically think: "What does that mean?" "It's because I'm a woman." "It's because of my ethnic background." "It's because I belong to a certain religious tradition." Maybe it's because you did something that was insensitive or hurtful. There may be many reasons, but once we let our fabricated self-image drop away, we can begin to understand people.

I once observed a very precocious two-year-old girl. When people asked her name, she would just look at them. When they asked her again, she would say, "I have no name." When they said, "Oh, surely you must have a name," she would say, "I've used them all up."

When she was older, this child asked me what causes thunder. I gave her the scientific answer meant for a preschool child and she said, "But what *causes* it?" So I explained it all again and she said, "But why? What *causes* it?" So I said, "It's caused by the dragons walking through the heavens," and she said, "Oh, that's it!" She was content with that explanation of the universe.

We can be either content or discontent, happy or unhappy. So why be unhappy? Usually we regard as positive those things which reinforce our concept of who we are, and as negative those things which either don't reinforce that concept or threaten it. These habit patterns are very difficult to break, but once I break them, I am not bothered even if someone launches a full-scale attack on me.

If others are making our life miserable, why let them win? Instead, we can look at ourselves and our idiosyncrasies, accept them, and learn to laugh at them. We learn to love ourselves with all our perceived strengths and all our perceived weaknesses. When I become angry, to feel guilty because I am not a fully enlightened Buddha is the height of egotism. On the phenomenological level, we are not Buddhas yet. When misunderstandings occurred, my teacher used to say, "Well, we're not Buddhas yet!" We need not expect ourselves to be Buddhas, nor expect our partners to be Buddhas either.

Situations of hurt need to be depersonalized so that the victim does not become burdened with guilt or shame. Healing cannot occur as long as we internalize events and blame ourselves. In a sense, in not understanding the essence of the mind, the perpetrator is also the victim. Rather than creating a separation between myself as victim and the other as perpetrator, we need to understand that each of us is capable of the most heinous acts. If you don't believe it, you have not explored yourself very well yet. Rather than deny it, we need to confront ourselves very directly. There are also countless ways in which we victimize ourselves.

By contrast, a bodhisattva, one who is truly on the path, has an invincible armor—the armor of love. The love of a bodhisattva is immeasurably great and we can glimpse it through intensive meditation. Such a being willingly endures lifetimes of suffering to save other beings. The bodhisattva path is wisdom and compassion—a path of choosing wisely, with love.

Chapter 7
Dealing with Stress

by Ayya Khema

How to deal with stress is a topic that concerns everyone, since we all have experienced the anxieties of daily living. In Buddhist terminology we don't necessarily call it stress, we just call it dukkha. Dukkha has different names and appears in many forms and guises. Dukkha is a Pali word and it is one for which we need a number of translations. Although dukkha is often translated as suffering, it also means dissatisfaction, unfulfillment, the niggling feeling inside that asks, "There must be something more in life. Where is it?" Then, after going off on a search for it and trying one thing after another, it's the feeling of still being unfulfilled. It's everything that we don't get when we want it and everything we get when we don't want it. That is dukkha in a nutshell, and stress is part of it.

We like to transfer the blame for our dukkha to scapegoats, such as the traffic, or the weather, the boss, or the high cost of living. Often we blame our neighbors, children, partner, or parents. Parents are popular scapegoats these days, but all of the scapegoats are popular—all in succession and all in constant rotation. Naturally we do have sickness, and not feeling well, and all the other assorted ills which beset humankind. As we look at our own dukkha, the immediate response for a non-practitioner, and at times for practitioners, too, is "There is something wrong. If I can set it right, I will get rid of my dukkha." So if I have stress, it must be, "I am working too hard, so I'll work two hours less each day and I won't have any more stress." Whoever has tried this knows it's nonsense. It doesn't work. A little more time to do other things might be gained, but that's all—the stress is not removed. When we experience dukkha of any kind, we are quick to find fault, always forgetting it is our own response that we are experiencing.

We have other ways of dealing with our dukkha, most just as ineffectual as blaming someone else. We may blame the circumstances of our lives, asking, "Why wasn't I born with a golden spoon in my mouth?" or "Why don't I have more understanding of the people around me?" Another way is to try and forget about the dukkha by distracting ourselves from it. We practice distraction with a vengeance. Television is number one on the list. Then we have the radio, the telephone, and conversations, whether needed or not. We have novels to read, and travel—the backpacker syndrome. Travel is made easy these days. Most of us can buy a ticket to wherever we would like to go, and once there, we are so busy changing our money, trying to find a place to sleep, trying to understand what people are saying, and buying souvenirs, that we get a lot of new dukkha and we forget about the old. Distraction is just another way we try to get out of dukkha.

Another related method is escape, or "trying to get away." Trying to get away can be physical or mental. Trying to get away is saying, "I want something changed, so I am going to change it. It must be the boss, or the people I work with, so I'll get a new job." Or, it may be "I'll change my partner," which is quite popular, too. We can't change our children. We are stuck with them, but we usually have the consolation that they are going to leave home one day. If it is not changing one's job or one's partner, it may be choosing a totally new job direction. It may be studying something, learning something, or moving somewhere, moving from the city to the country and growing one's own carrots. Then, of course, it's getting sick and tired of that and moving back to the city. Sometimes we move to a different country, thinking "Maybe the people in another country know better what to do." So we try to remove ourselves physically. Sometimes we dye our hair. It doesn't help much, but it is a change. We can diet, or learn exercises and feel like a new person, or use crystals, or whatever happens to be popular at the moment.

Then, of course, we try to remove ourselves mentally. We just cut ourselves off. We dislike the whole situation and in order to avoid our dukkha, we become indifferent. We distance ourselves from our emotions. We don't pay attention to what is really happening. Of course, none of this is a solution. It is all just a reaction. I compare this reaction to a jack-in-the-box. A jack-in-the-box is a toy for children, with a little doll that sits on a spring inside a box, and there is a lid on the box, and when the child touches the lid, the little doll jumps out. Imagine for a moment that somebody comes along and removes the little doll from the box. The child can hit the lid with a hammer, but nothing will jump out. It is the same with us. We all have a jack-in-the-box inside that needs our attention. That is the Buddha's teaching. He doesn't call it a jack-in-the-box, but he tells us to attend to what is going on inside. When we do, we will see the whole world change, because we will change the way we react. This applies to all of our dukkha, no matter what it is.

We talk of the stress and strain of modern living, but I don't think there is anything modern about stress. I think we have always had it. Trying to get results is the worst of the stress. We put pressure on ourselves. We have a certain idea about ourselves, about how we should be and how we should have success, how others should see us, how others should appreciate and support us. And with this image we have of ourselves, we cannot come to the truth of ourselves. Our self-image might say, "I am clever, young and beautiful." Or it might say, "I am stupid, old, and ugly." Usually the image we have of ourselves is balanced. We might think, "Well, I am not so beautiful, but I am clever," or, "I am not as young as I used to be, but I can still do everything I need to do." We try to balance it out. With this image, we want a support system for the person we think we are. We want to think that person is not only there, but is also okay. That person is fine—everything is working well. Now obviously, no one has that kind of success. Not even the Buddha was loved and liked by everyone. Certainly Jesus wasn't; he was killed for his pains.

So, we look for a support system everywhere and from everyone, because we want to get results, whether success in business, success in marriage, or just harmony around us. We dislike it when whatever we are looking for doesn't happen. We call that stress.

Stress is not having a lot to do. People who are completely mindful, paying total attention without judgment, can go from one activity to the next without feeling stressed. Mindfulness does not allow for judgments such as, "Am I successful or not?" Mindfulness only allows for complete attention. Mindfulness is the heart of the Buddha's teaching in all respects. It is the first of the Seven Factors of Enlightenment and the seventh stage of the Eightfold Noble Path. The Buddha said, "Mindfulness is as essential as salt to the curry."

The one who is mindful will find happiness everywhere. Mindfulness is not just a word. It is a mental activity and unless we have it, we cannot get rid of stress. Stress arises from not getting the support, appreciation, and success that we are looking for. Disliking this situation entirely, we feel less and less energetic in getting on with what we need to be doing. The more negative we are, the more stress we feel. It is just plain old dukkha in another disguise. We have to hurry to get to work, but instead of having the idea that there has to be a result from it, we just do it. Simple, isn't it? This has to be learnt, and everybody and anybody can learn it. It is not that we no longer do our best. On the contrary, we do our very best and that's it. We have no jurisdiction over results which arise from the situation, the activity, the people, or other factors outside ourself. Having done what is appropriate in the situation—whatever that may be—we have the satisfaction of knowing we have tried our best. Sometimes the mind says, "Couldn't you have done a little better?" Apparently not, otherwise we would have done it.

Constant criticism, constant judgment, and constant self-hatred obviously bring about stress. How can it be otherwise? If I feel aversion, if I feel negative, if I have hatred, if I have criticism, judgment or fear of not being successful, the mind becomes tense and the tension creates more stress. The stress then creates more tension, in an ever-turning, ever-increasing circle. In order to break out of this pattern, the first thing to do is to meditate every day—morning and night—and to join in a group meditation once a week. It is essential that we look after our own minds. Where is stress? Stress is in the mind, isn't it? Stress eventually manifests in the body, too, but it starts in the mind. If we have any inkling of spiritual practice, Buddhist or otherwise, we must realize that it is our mind we need to look after.

We are all very skillful at looking after the body, and there is nothing wrong in that. We know how to feed it. We know how to give it a rest. We know that it needs some exercise. We know to give it medicine when it's sick. We must, however, be equally skillful in looking after the mind—in fact, more skillful. Mind is the master. The first verse of the *Dhammapada*, a collection of the verses of the Buddha, begins with this topic. If we take a moment to examine our mind, we can only agree that the mind is the key. Certainly the body experiences pain, discomfort and disease, but what reacts to it is the mind. Stress is in our mind, so if we want to reduce or eliminate stress, we have to look after the mind. We need to make the mind a tool that is so sharp and clear that it will do what we want it to do and not just be a trigger mechanism that responds to the innumerable outer provocations.

Recently, being driven through London, I realized that the triggers for stress are at every corner, at every car. Suddenly someone decides to make a left turn, right in front of us, and doesn't even give a signal. Then we want to make a turn, but it's a one-way street, and we have an appointment. We are supposed to be there at four o'clock. It produces stress if we let it, but why let it? Why allow it?

One of the things that helps enormously is to remember our own death. Death could happen at any moment. Does anyone have a written guarantee that they are going to be around next year, next week, or tomorrow? What is important between now and one's death? Certainly it's not important to get upset or to get stressed out by all the happenings around us. What's more important? Is it that stress, or finding inner peace and harmony?

A very helpful thing to do, something I advise in meditation courses, is to take a piece of paper and pencil, and write down what we want to do with our life, starting now. We ask ourselves, "What am I going to do with the rest of my life, which is just beginning this moment? What is most important? What am I really looking for? What do I want? Do I want to continue to get upset and worried? Do I want to hope for the best or remember the worst? Do I want to change something?" We write it all down and when it stares us in the face from the blank piece of paper, it hits home. We realize that maybe that isn't what we want. Maybe we want something else. And when we realize what we really want to do, we realize that we have to look after the mind.

We have to be just as careful with our mind as we are with our body. We don't voluntarily eat anything that is spoiled, rotten, or poisonous. Are we watching our mind in the same way? Do we ever take anything into the mind which is spoiled, rotten, or poisonous? Every negativity that enters our mind is a great detriment to our well-being. Negativity could be called poisonous. Whether we think negatively about ourselves or others doesn't make the slightest difference. We have an image of ourselves and others as near perfection, which is absurd, since only an enlightened being can be perfect. Having an image of near or total perfection brings dissatisfaction, since we see imperfections, and dislike what we see. We start disliking ourselves and disliking everybody else as well. Then, of course, we feel stress and strain because things don't go harmoniously, but how could they?

We would like things in our life to be different, but is that wish really going to make any difference? The only difference we can actually make is when we change ourselves. When that jack-in-the-box no longer immediately responds to everything that touches us, things can be different. With some people all you have to do is touch the lid very lightly and jack-in-the-box jumps out. For others you have to hit a little harder, but usually a response comes. If we really want to change our lives and the world, we have got to change ourselves and our responses. We might like to change our partner, but there is only one person we can change, and that is ourselves.

We have the potential for enlightenment. Each one of us has the seed of enlightenment within. Otherwise, the Buddha would have taught in vain for forty-five years. But all the debris of our thoughts and emotions covers up that beautiful spark within. Subconsciously we know that it is there, that there is no need to look outside of ourselves. It is not to be found in temples or churches. It is within our own heart. We all know it, but we don't dare acknowledge it.

Why? Because we are wasting our lives. It is as simple as that. We have come in this human form with all our senses and limbs intact, with the opportunity to hear the true Dharma, with the best possible opportunity, and if we don't use this opportunity for the best of pursuits, it is a great waste of human potential. Enlightenment might sound like a tall order, and it is, so we start with something smaller. We sit down and meditate.

Why does meditation help us to look after the mind? First, meditation is the only way the mind can get a rest. All day long we think, emote, and react. All night long we dream. This most beautiful and valuable of all tools, our own mind, never gets a moment's rest. The only way it can get a rest is when we sit down and concentrate on a meditation subject. Second, meditation is the main way of purification. One moment of concentration is one moment of purification. Stress will always be there, particularly in a big city, but the purified mind no longer needs to react to it. In a big city, everyone is rushing from one place to the next . . . even watching it is stressful. Stress will always be there, but we don't have to suffer from it. Day in and day out we wash and clean our body, and yet that is all we clean. We also need to purify the mind and give it a rest. The Buddha said that one way of purification is mindfulness. Mindfulness means focusing the mind on one thing, being one-pointed. In meditation we have to be mindful of the meditation subject. This way we purify the mind and give it new energy. When we see our thoughts and emotions arise in meditation, eventually we can just watch them arise and cease, and don't have to react to them.

In everyday life, when our mind says, "This is terrible, this is stressful. I have got to do something about it. I am going to change my job," or "I am going to sell the car," or "I have got to move to the country," we know that we are just reacting. We realize that stress is in the reactions of our own mind.

When we sit and meditate, we choose a time when everything is quiet and we expect not to be disturbed. We sit quietly, but we can't concentrate. Anyone who has tried it knows. Why can't we keep our mind on the breath? What is the mind doing? As we watch it, we will see that the mind has a tendency to think, to react, to emote, and to fantasize. It does everything under the sun except concentrate. We become very aware of that in meditation and we have to change it, otherwise we can't meditate. So we substitute all that is going on in the mind with attention on the breath, again and again. We learn to substitute positive reactions for our negative reactions.

No matter what we see as our greatest difficulty, we realize that it is our dislike of it that makes us suffer. The world is never going to be all right. The big cities are never going to be quiet. The neighbors are never going to turn the radio off. The dogs are not going to stop barking. And the traffic in London is going to increase, not decrease, that is for sure. So why worry about it? That is just the way it is. So why not worry about what goes on within?

We make our lives miserable by being miserable, so why not do exactly the opposite, and make our lives happy, joyful, and harmonious, by being happy, joyful, and harmonious? We create our own lives and yet we think that something else is doing it. All we have to do is change our mental reactions towards the opposite direction. And the way to do that is to meditate, otherwise we won't have the strength of mind to do it. A mind that can meditate is a mind that is one-pointed. And a mind that is one-pointed, the Buddha said, is like an ax that has been sharpened. It has a sharp edge that can cut through everything. If we want to remove stress and strain, and have a different quality of life, we have every opportunity. We need to strengthen our mind to the point where it will not suffer from the things which exist in the world.

The Buddha expressed his enlightenment in the Four Noble Truths, under the famous bodhi tree in what is now Bodhgaya. The first and second noble truths concern dukkha. The first one says that existence is dukkha and unsatisfactory. The second one says that the only cause of dukkha is craving, wanting. What do we want? We want things to be the way we think they ought to be, but there are five billion others who think exactly the same way, so that doesn't work, does it? Eventually we start to practice a spiritual path and to live a spiritual life. A spiritual path and a spiritual life are directly opposed to a worldly life and a materialistic life, but only inwardly. We can continue to wear the same clothes, live in the same place, have the same job, and the same family around us. The difference does not lie in the outer trappings. The difference lies in one essential fact. On the worldly path we want to get whatever it is we are looking for, whether it is peace, harmony, love, support, appreciation, money, success, or whatever. And as long as we want something—anything—we will have dukkha. We will have stress. That is the meaning of the first and second noble truths.

The difference in being on the spiritual path is that we give up the wanting. If we can give up the wanting, there can be no stress. If we can see that difference, if we can see that without the "me wanting" there can be no stress, then we can continue on the path. Naturally, we cannot give up all our wanting all at once; there will be stages. But we can give up trying to change the outer conditions and instead begin changing the inner ones. This is not so difficult, but we do need meditation.

One thing we can do is think for a moment, "What is it that I do not like about my life?" Whatever comes to mind, we drop it. For one moment, we drop the dislike of the other person or the situation that has come to mind. We can pick it up again the next moment and have the whole dislike back if we want to, but just drop it for one moment and see the relief. If we can do that over and over again, we realize that our lives are the effects of causes that we ourselves have set into motion, an example of karma and its results. We realize that each situation presented to us is a learning situation on a spiritual path.

If we ever ask ourselves, "What is life all about? What are we here for?" we can truthfully answer by saying, "It is an adult education class, and that is all." Some people have the mistaken view that it is an amusement park, that if we pay enough entrance fee, we can enjoy all the amusements around, but that is a mistaken view. Adult education is extremely valuable and very interesting. Why not use life for that? The whole of daily life is nothing but lessons on not blaming anyone, including ourselves. Instead we just see the situation as it is. We need to stop running away from the situation, trying to cover it over with distractions, and start looking at it thinking, "What am I learning from this?" Sometimes the situations are very unpleasant, but the more unpleasant they are, the more we can learn from them. If we don't learn from them, we can be sure that the same situations will arise again. The people will have different names, but it will be the same story all over again. Just as in school, if we don't pass the exams the first time, we have to sit through the classes again. If we don't understand what we are being taught, we have to be taught again.

If we thought we were finished with learning when we left school, we were mistaken. School was only the beginning. What they taught us in school was only how to cope with making a living, and that is just one small part of life. The rest we are learning from day to day. The more we learn, the easier it gets. Wisdom comes through understood experience.

Dukkha arises because we don't like the way things are. We don't have to like things the way they are, but we can like the way they teach us something. We can have gratitude for every teaching, and then we won't feel stressed. We feel buoyant and everything becomes so much easier. Meditation is a means to that end.

Chapter 8

Abortion: A Respectful Meeting Ground

by Yvonne Rand

American attitudes about abortion have given birth to heart-breaking polarization and violence. The need for a safe and respectful meeting ground for everyone concerned now overrides the issues themselves. My own view on the issues may seem inconsistent on the surface, for I am anti-abortion and pro-choice, but what most concerns me these days are the intolerance and intemperance which prevent any harmony between the contending camps. I see remarkable grief in people as an aftermath of abortions and miscarriages and no container in which to heal that grief.

The perspective on abortion I present here has developed through my experiences as a practicing Buddhist and a Zen priest, as a woman, and as a mother. In conducting memorial ceremonies under the benevolent auspices of Jizo Bodhisattva, I have come to appreciate the capacity the Buddhadharma has to show us how to develop our ability to hold and to accept what is painful and difficult. In Japan, Jizo is the much-loved form of the Bodhisattva of the underworld; he is the emanation of compassion who guides and protects transmigrators into and out of life.

My first encounter with Jizo Bodhisattva took place in 1969 after a dear friend of mine died in a train accident in Japan. Several years earlier, my friend had gone on a search for himself which ended in a Japanese Zen monastery. His sudden death was a blow and I grieved his passing deeply. Later that year I found myself driving Suzuki Roshi to Tassajara Zen Mountain Center from San Francisco. When I told him that I had been taking care of a foot-locker holding my friend's precious belongings (music, a flute, essays, books, drawings), Suzuki Roshi suggested that we burn the belongings in the stone garden near his cabin at Tassajara. After a proper funeral and fire ceremony, we buried the ashes in the rock garden, and marked the spot with a small stone figure of Jizo.

This, my first meeting with Jizo, affected me deeply. For some years afterwards, I could not explain my pull to the figure of this sweet-faced monk with hands in the mudra of prayer and greeting.

Several years after this funeral ceremony, I terminated an unexpected pregnancy by having an abortion. I suffered after the abortion, but it was not until some years had passed that I came to understand fully either my grieving or the resolution to which I eventually came.

Subsequently, I began spending time in Japan and became reacquainted with Jizo. Figures of Jizo are everywhere there. I saw firsthand that Jizo ritual and ceremony involved not just graveyards and death in general but particularly the deaths of infants and fetuses through abortion, miscarriage or stillbirth. Back home, during the seventies and eighties, women had begun coming to me and asking if I could help them with their difficulties in the aftermath of an abortion or a miscarriage. In consequence I began doing a simple memorial service for groups of people who had experienced the death of fetuses and babies. After many years of counseling both men and women, I decided, four years ago, to spend several months in Japan doing a focused study of the Jizo practices.

Initially I did the ceremony only with women. But now I include men and children as well. The participants are neither all pro-choice nor all pro-life in their politics; a full spectrum of opinion and belief is represented in the circle we make. Many of the people who come are not Buddhists. Yet somehow this old Buddhist way seems to absorb whoever does come.

What the ceremony accomplishes is to provide a means for people to be with what is so, no matter how painful that may be. Being fundamentally awake to what is so is a great path, open to us all. The path means awakening to what is truly and specifically so, rather than remaining narcotized or habitually preoccupied by our fears and desires, our loves and hates. Ignorance and unconsciousness make us lose our way and cause great suffering to ourselves and others. Sex, as we know, can lead to pregnancy. Failure to consider the gestative potential of sexuality can result in suffering for one's entire lifetime, and for the lifetime of all those involved. Women who have had abortions are sometimes haunted for decades afterwards.

All those who attend our ceremonies have suffered the death of one or more small beings. Strangers assemble with their grief and unresolved dismay. Over time I have been struck by how successfully the ceremony has provided a container for the process of acknowledging what is so, for encompassing what is difficult, and for bringing about resolution and healing.

When I initially performed the Buddhist Memorial Ceremony, I followed a quite traditional form. Slowly I have modified and added to it in a way that seems to work better for Americans.

The ceremony is as follows: We sit in silence, sewing a bib or hat for one of the compassion figures on the altar. The figures are from different cultures: Jizo, Mary with Jesus, "Spirit entering and leaving" from the Eskimo people, or a mother and child. Our commitment is to listen to those who wish to talk without attempting to give advice or comfort. Some of us know from twelve-step meetings of the important practice of simply listening. The principle of "no cross-talk" provides safety from uninvited comforting and solicitude, and many find it to be the most healing of possible attentions. After this, we walk to the garden, form a circle, and go through a simple ceremony of acknowledging a particular life and death. One by one, each person says whatever is in his or her heart while offering incense, placing the sewn garments on one of the altar figures, and bowing. We then chant the *Heart Sutra*, giving the unborn beings Dharma names and saying good-bye to them. Prayer sticks are made and inscribed with prayers for forgiveness and for the well-being of those who have died. No names are signed. The prayers are hung from the bushes and trees in the meditation garden, thus committing our messages to the wind and the rains. Afterwards we have a cup of tea, walk in the garden, and go home with a quieter heart.

Some years ago, at a conference for women in Buddhism, I led the Jizo ceremony for a large group of conference participants. At the end of the ceremony a woman spoke about her own experience. She described herself as a nurse midwife who did a lot of abortion counseling. After her own abortion she began to ask the women who came to her for help first to go home and talk to the fetus they were carrying. She encouraged them to tell the baby all the reasons for their inner conflict about the pregnancy. She reported that the number of spontaneous miscarriages that occurred was remarkable. After hearing her story I began to hear about a similar practice of speaking to the fetus in other cultures: in Cambodia, in the Netherlands, and among native peoples in America, for example. I find great sense in this practice. Speaking to the fetal baby is a way to recognize and acknowledge that the being *in utero* also is a presence, also has a voice, also has some concern for the outcome. I continue to be struck by the deep rightness of such an attitude in the midst of the suffering that comes with conflict over a pregnancy.

I have added modern touches to the ceremony. Yet the wisdom it embraces comes from traditional Buddhist teachings, which, although steeped in history, nevertheless offer profound guidance for the current conflict over abortion. For me, the Buddha's first grave precept—not to kill intentionally—cannot be denied, much less minimized. Since I am convinced that the teaching embodied in the precept is correct, both conventionally and ultimately, and since adherence to it is a necessary step on the path that leads away from suffering, I feel compelled to take a stand against abortion.

At the same time, I can readily and willingly keep someone company when abortion is the choice she has arrived at. I am strongly in favor of the freedom of each individual to choose for herself what to do regarding a conflicted pregnancy. I could not and would not advocate a return to the years when the government controlled the woman's decision. In 1955, when abortion was illegal, almost one out of four American women had an abortion by the age of forty-five, and some perished in the process.

What, then, is the solution? My experience as a Buddhist priest continues to teach me that looking into a situation in detail, without glossing over what is unpleasant or difficult, is what helps us to stay present and clear and to break through ignorance. This is certainly true in the potent realms of sexuality, fertility, and gestation. The premise of restraint, which underlies all the Buddha's precepts and is fundamental in the practice of compassion, is also of critical importance in how we lead our sexual lives. Through the precepts and through the practice of awareness of what is so, we can understand our previous actions and make wise decisions about future actions. By contrast, action which is based on unexamined and habitual thought patterns—implanted in childhood and reinforced by the generalities, platitudes and superficialities of the common culture—perpetuate ignorance and sentence us to ever-renewing suffering.

The solution I propose is neither tidy nor quick. I have seen that there is no easy or "right" answer. I think that each woman must stay with her experience and be with what is so in as simple and clear a way as she can. I feel that it is important, whatever one's starting point on the abortion issue, to study its history in this nation. By doing so, we will benefit from a wider framework and a more open point of view.[1]

Chapter 9
Buddhism and the Twelve Steps

by Rachel V.

I sat in the meditation hall at 5:00 A.M. The temperature was just below freezing. The cobalt-blue wood-burning stove was crackling mightily, but at the other end of the zendo, providing me with absolutely no heat. I had a roaring headache, was angry, nauseous, and hungover. I was a Buddhist alcoholic.

I began studying Buddhism to get my life under control. Why wasn't it working? After my evening run to the woods and back, how could I have stayed out drinking again? I knew better. I was a single mother. I had children to care for, meals to fix, bathing and homework to supervise, bedtime stories to tell, songs to sing...at least that's what I intended to do. How could this have happened again?

Two early morning periods of zazen gave me plenty of time to experience the effects of my increasingly unpredictable drinking. The pounding in my head, the queasy feeling in my stomach, and the exhaustion all mounted, and were intensified by the three closing bows at the end of the meditation. If I had been drinking the night before, the morning service would leave me reeling, nearly falling over as I bent my knees, raised my hands, and leaned over to touch my head to the wooden floor in the traditional bow.

There were many mornings when I was clear-headed. I loved the peacefulness of the meditation hall and being with the community of other students. I loved the growing light as sunrise filled the room, spreading down the soft white walls in the zendo. With the sun, the birds' songs began, a seaside breeze picked up, and the boughs of the old Monterey pine next to the zendo scratched the corrugated tin roof with a reassuring sound.

Sometimes in the evenings, I would go for a run, jogging home to be with my children before supper. Sometimes, despite all my best intentions and promises to myself and my children, I would stop at our neighborhood pub, just for a glass or two of white wine or beer, to chat with a neighbor or some of the Zen students who frequented the pub in our neighborhood. Sometimes I would stop drinking at one or two glasses, but sometimes I wouldn't. The moment of crossing the invisible line that stands between enjoyment and intoxication began to evade me with increasing frequency.

Sitting zazen in the zendo every morning and doing mindfulness practices helped me to generate an awareness of my drinking, but did not get me sober. As my addiction progressed, I was thinking about when I could drink and how much I could drink, even when I wasn't drinking. I made elaborate bargains with myself. If I had done two periods of meditation in the morning, run three miles in the evening, and written eight pages on the story I was writing, then I could have two glasses of wine as a reward--but only two. When I violated these interior bargains that I had made with myself, I not only became terrified, but also angry with myself and my family. Why wasn't my willpower working? I was increasingly plagued by shame and self-loathing. My downward spiral had begun.

One night I arrived home late and was confronted by my fierce thirteen-year-old daughter. When I asked her to bring me just one more glass of wine, she refused. This was the moment of clarity. Time stopped. Buddhism had helped ready me for this moment: I suddenly knew that my only choice was to admit that I am an alcoholic. I knew I either had to ask for help, or drink myself to an alcoholic suicidal death. I got on the phone and called for help. My recovery began that night. It was a great relief to finally acknowledge that I had no power over alcohol. I knew I could no longer pretend to be in control of my drinking or my life.

The seduction of alcoholism had grown with time. Repeating the experience of having one or two drinks and sometimes being able to stop, other times not, was like gambling or Russian roulette. There was a rush of excitement with the danger, the risk I knew I was taking. Yet the terror of completely losing control also grew. It seemed that something, something not particularly friendly or beneficial, inhabited my body. That entity, "the disease," had its own agenda.

Gregory Bateson talked about alcohol as a folk-remedy for schizophrenia. My experience told me that alcoholism *produces* schizophrenia instead. Recovery, for me, has been a process of acknowledging and befriending a "divided self." The study of Buddhism, especially, has helped me to see that the concept of a "divided self," or even a "self," is an illusion. Thus Buddhism and the twelve steps concur that self-centeredness is the root of all troubles.

The illusion that I could control my drinking was the ultimate seduction that took me to the depths. Yet the bottom turned out not to be the end, as I had feared, but the beginning, a passageway into a transformative way of life. The discipline of the daily practice of sobriety initiates a spiritual awakening. This awakening enables us to turn away from craving the anesthesia of alcohol or drugs.

Initially, it seemed to me that Buddhism and the twelve-step program of Alcoholics Anonymous were very different. The twelfth step is a clear directive to develop a spiritual practice, but while Buddhism is non-theistic, AA meetings are often filled with talk of God or a "higher power." This seemed a flat contradiction. The languages of Buddhism are precise, elegant, piercing, and beautiful, whereas the language of AA meetings can be downright offensive. Some meetings were painful to sit through. I wanted to think that I was different because I was a Buddhist. I often wanted to bolt out the door screaming, but I always stopped myself. Where would I go? Whether or not I approved of the AA language or its epistemology, or the gender exclusivity of its *Big Book*,[1] I realized that the people I met in AA knew about staying sober and I did not.

I came to this realization slowly. I did not want to be in AA in the beginning, thinking it meant I had failed as a student of Buddhism and wouldn't measure up to my Buddhist brothers and sisters. Over the years I stopped looking for ways to defend myself against the program. I began to give up my judgments. As I became more open and less defensive, the changes in other people began to astonish me. The insights they shared in meetings were as rich and meaningful as any koan, and sometimes even more so, since they were fully embodied in the transformed people standing before me.

All of this happened more than eleven years ago. Now, as a student of both Buddhism and what I call "the practice of sobriety," I feel quite differently about the disparity I imagined between Buddhist practice and the twelve steps. It has proved to be imaginary. My own guilt and shame are gone. Initially, I hoped that one day I would just "get well" and not have to go to any more meetings. Couldn't I just do my Buddhist practice and maintain my sobriety? Now I can't imagine one practice without the other. I enjoy AA meetings and sitting zazen. Buddhism and the twelve steps have become integrated so completely in my view, that I call them "the Formless Form."

Over the years I've discovered that the AA twelve steps are themselves a rigorous form of Dharma, the community of recovery another form of Sangha, and the power of people telling the truth about their lives at the meetings, a manifestation of the Buddha potentiality that lies within us all. Buddhism has opened doors for me, doors into an unlimited universe of spiritual practices. The twelve steps have given me down-to-earth, practical tools for living life without alcohol or drugs, one day at a time. The commonality of the two practices becomes more apparent as the years pass.

Both Buddhism and the twelve steps have service to others as the ultimate purpose of life. *The Big Book* states it quite simply. The main object "is to enable you to find a Power greater than yourself...." Spiritual experience is central, as the twelfth step expresses: "Having had a spiritual awakening as a result of these steps, we tried to carry this message to alcoholics, and to practice these principles in all our affairs."

Alcoholism is just one form of addiction. We can be addicted to behaviors as well as to substances. Bernie Glassman Sensei of the Zen Community of New York goes further and says, "We're ego addicts, all of us." Christine Longaker, a senior student of the Vajrayana teacher Sogyal Rinpoche, maintains that we're all addicted to samsara. Struck by the efficacy of the twelve steps with people who had been students of Buddhism for years, a small group of Sogyal's students in Seattle have begun to investigate the interface between the two forms. More and more people, both Buddhists and twelve-step practitioners, are becoming aware of the parallels between these two systems.

In *The Big Book* we are told that the "real purpose [of recovery] is to fit ourselves to be of maximum service to God and the people about us." With the ideal of bodhichitta, Buddhism provides an even larger context for this principle of selflessness, making possible a cosmic, intergalactic view. We seek to become enlightened for the sake of all beings, in all times, in all places.

> May I and all living beings in the three worlds
> Be able to see the faults of the evils of the self-grasping attitude
>   which binds us to existence.
> Bestow your blessings so that I may cut the root of samsara
> With the sharp weapon of the wisdom which understands
>   selflessness.[2]

The Buddha taught that only this moment is real. The vast and completely empty *now* is lived out and relied upon in twelve-step practice in a way not often encountered in other places. Perhaps the fruits of twelve-step programs are so abundantly evident because the changes in people's lives, even in physical appearance, can be so dramatic. An alcoholic/addict in recovery lives on the edge, beneath the sword of Damocles. In a life of sobriety, there are no more hiding places. The AA *Big Book*, the acknowledged authority upon which the twelve-step programs are built, tells us: "What we really have is a daily reprieve contingent on the maintenance of our spiritual condition." This sounded melodramatic to me until I was sober a few years. Some people drank and came back to AA. Some continued drinking and never came back. I knew people who drank or used again and died, seemingly, in my experience, by suicide. Relapse often happens, whether people are sober for thirty days or thirty years. So far I have chosen not to lose my sobriety and risk having to start over again.

The structure of AA meetings is grounded in the belief that if people come together to share their experience, their strengths, and their hopes, this will help them stay sober, one day at a time. We leave aside talk of politics, career, and religion, hold no property, charge no money, demand no adherence to a belief system, allow no interruption of someone speaking, but only respectful listening. We admit to something greater than the individuals in the group and allow it to work in people's lives. This "something larger" can be called the Buddha nature, God, or simply a higher power. Each individual can decide what to call it, if they call it anything at all. There are no vows. People stay sober, if they do, one day at a time. No one is a senior member. There are no abbots, no teachers, no appointed leaders, only rotating secretaries who serve for six months, hence the wisdom in everyone is tapped. Experience, strength, and hope are shared with generosity. No advice is given, other than to accept oneself and others.

As the streams of Buddhism and the twelve steps continue to flow into American society, it becomes increasingly evident that Buddhism and the twelve steps are beginning to influence each other in ways that may shape Buddhism in North America for years to come. Just as Buddhism incorporated elements of Hinduism in India, the Bon tradition in Tibet, and Taoism in China, it may be that Buddhism will incorporate elements of the twelve-step movement in America.

Chapter 10
Karma: Creative Responsibility

Karma Lekshe Tsomo

Women have traditionally borne a special responsibility for imparting moral values to successive generations of children. There are also many modern ethical issues that are of particular concern to women. As the bearers and nurturers of children, women must make decisions concerning contraception, adoption, and abortion, for example. As caregivers to the elderly, the lonely, the terminally ill, and pets, they are faced with the issues of euthanasia and assisted suicide. As homemakers, they are confronted daily with the issue of killing insects and must bear the burden of decisions concerning insecticides and fumigation.

Paradoxically, in the Buddhist view, the achieving of human perfection rests upon our understanding that we lack true existence. Liberation is thus simultaneously a matter of self-realization and realization of non-self. A person engages in actions, positive and negative, lifetime after lifetime, until liberated from cyclic existence, yet no trace of a person passes from life to life. By dispelling all attachments, aversions, and delusions from the mind, particularly the delusion of being a truly existent person, the person actualizes her or his maximum potential.

In contrast to earlier Indian systems of thought, the Buddha rejected the notion of an independent self or soul. It is due to ignorance and delusion that we mistakenly perceive a self to exist where it does not. Clinging to notions of "I" and "mine," we create unwholesome actions with unhappy results. This process can be reversed through meditation. Realizing selflessness eliminates the basis for clinging to people, possessions, and to existence itself. With no substratum, no self to defend or promote, the delusions of attachment, hatred, and confusion find nowhere to root. Without the delusions, we avoid unwholesome actions and their unfortunate results. Thus, an understanding of selflessness is the foundation for moral perfection and the key to liberation. By developing the wisdom realizing selflessness, no longer seeing self and others as objects of attachment or aversion, we eventually achieve nirvana, or liberation from the miserable process of repeated rebirth.

In the Buddhist system there is no one sitting in judgment, no punishing God, and no one dictating right and wrong. Instead, there is the Noble Eightfold Path of right view, right intention, right speech, right action, right livelihood, right effort, right mindfulness, and right concentration based upon an understanding of the impersonal law of cause and effect, known as karma. Just as mango seeds give rise to mango trees and chili seeds give rise to chili plants, wholesome deeds lead to happiness while unwholesome deeds lead to suffering. Since everyone wants to be happy and no one wants to suffer, it stands to reason that we should strive to avoid unwholesome actions and create wholesome ones. Buddhism does not decree absolute right or wrong, but leaves individuals free to determine for themselves the appropriate course of action in the particular circumstances. Thus Buddhism presents an ethic of personal choice and responsibility, based on an understanding of cause and effect, and informed by compassion and wisdom.

The crucial element in Buddhist ethical theory is intention. What is the motive behind the action? The Burmese lay teacher U. S. N. Goenka uses the example of a thief who kills someone with a knife during a robbery and a doctor who kills someone with a knife during surgery. In both cases the action, killing a human being, and the result of the action, the death of a human being, are the same. What differs is the motivation behind the action. If the thief's motivation is greed and anger, the consequences of the action for the thief will be seriously negative. If the doctor's motivation is compassion and the preserving of life, the consequences of the action for the doctor will be positive. When we evaluate our actions in this light, we understand more clearly the difference between, for example, scolding a child with compassion and scolding a child with anger. We see that careless chatter is less serious than malicious gossip, accidental shortchanging less serious than premeditated theft. Since actions of body and speech proceed from the mind, we understand the importance of motivation in understanding the law of cause and effect.

Buddhist moral philosophy is strikingly pragmatic. Something is valuable insofar as it is relevant to people's lives and useful for achieving their happiness. If it will bring happiness for oneself and others, pursue it; if it will bring suffering, better to avoid it. There are no absolute dictates; ethical personal behavior is seen as simply the most practical way to cope with the difficulties of the human condition. Although guidelines and copious illustrations are given, nothing is absolute or definitive. The power and freedom to make decisions rests with the individual. There is no arbitrary or mysterious force controlling our lives; there is simply the law of cause and effect. Of course, decisions are dependent upon many factors. The choices we make are conditioned by circumstances, both outer and inner, but ultimately human beings have free will to decide. Individuals make decisions and experience the consequences of their decisions.

Buddhist moral philosophy steers a middle path. With the aim of preventing pain and problematic situations, it avoids both extreme asceticism and licentious self-indulgence. We are the free agents of the actions we create, and we reap the rewards of our actions, both positive and negative. The motivation, or intention, behind our actions is crucial. If we accidentally step on an insect or hit a bird on the highway, we are the agent of the action, but we did not intend harm. Thus the impact of the action upon our mental continuum is far less serious than in the case of premeditated killing. When we drive carefully to avoid hitting animals and clean the kitchen counter mindfully to avoid harming insects, our intention is good and so, usually, is the result. Occasionally an ant may run into the sponge, but at least we tried our best.

The process of karma, explaining how actions reach fruition in this and future lives, is extremely complex. Since no two actions are identical in all aspects, the exact results of actions are difficult to predict. We can understand the broad outlines of the process, but it is said that only a perfectly enlightened Buddha sees karma in all its ramifications. The enlightened wisdom of a Buddha understands all things as they are, including the reason for every color in a peacock's tail, while unawakened beings flounder in cyclic existence, creating actions heedlessly. The working of karma is subtle: since there is no soul, abiding self, or permanent mind, actions make impressions on the mind-stream, the constantly changing stream of consciousness, that eventually ripen, giving rise to their result.

Our present actions are a mirror image of our thoughts and intentions. They are also like a mirror that reflects our future. If our lives are governed by selfishness, hatred, and anger, our future will be the natural outcome of those attitudes. If our lives are full of compassion, generosity, joy, and wisdom, our future will naturally correspond. We do not need to consult a fortune-teller or the Tarot cards; we can know our future from the quality of our present everyday life.

Observing the ten virtues of body, speech, and mind is a way of avoiding unwholesome actions. These ten are: to refrain from taking life, stealing, sexual misconduct; from dishonest, divisive, harsh, or frivolous speech; and from covetous, malicious, or wrong views. Pursuing the ten virtues, their opposites, is a means of wholesome character development that brings happiness by freeing us from fear, hatred, and regret. Guilt is replaced by psychological assets like concentration, joy, and insight. In this way, sound moral principles are transformative, facilitating rapid spiritual growth. We verify the theory through our own life experience.

One becomes a Buddhist by taking refuge in the Three Jewels: the Buddha, Dharma, and Sangha. The next level of commitment is becoming a Buddhist lay follower by undertaking to train in the five precepts. Training in the five precepts means making a conscious effort to refrain from killing, stealing, lying (especially about one's spiritual attainments), sexual misconduct, and intoxicants.

Any discussion of the first precept entails formulating a definition of life and the taking of life. Life, in this connection, has traditionally been defined as "sentient" life and beings with minds as "sentient beings." Since enlightenment is a possibility for all beings with minds, sentient life is regarded as precious. Sentient beings include hell beings, heavenly beings, ghosts, animals, and humans, but not rocks and plants. Since deities and spirits may live in association with plants, plants may react to stimuli, but in the early tradition, they do not have consciousness. The aspiration to "enlighten every blade of grass" expressed in later traditions may be a poetic metaphor.

Whereas the commandment "Thou shalt not kill" is ordinarily interpreted to mean "Thou shalt not kill *humans*," the Buddhist perspective includes all forms of animal life as well. To refrain from killing means to abstain from killing any sentient being, including even cockroaches and ants. Each living creature is as attached to its life as any other, as we can see when they scurry away. In institutions such as the Society for the Prevention of Cruelty to Animals and in sayings such as "She's so kind, she wouldn't kill a fly," we see that the notion of non-harm often extends to non-human life forms in Western culture, too. Thus, Buddhism reaffirms some of our own cultural ideals.

Our attitudes on social and ethical issues are reflections of our personal worldview. Conditioned by our upbringing and education, these attitudes are also impermanent. Previous opinions, even our entire worldview, may change with time and experience. An example is the major advance in human consciousness made in recent years due to increasing feminist awareness, which is making an impact on all aspects of society, politics, and ethics. Yet even among feminists there is a wide range of opinion.

For instance, feminists typically affirm the inherent worth of all human beings, yet many find themselves on opposite ends of the spectrum when it comes to an issue like abortion. Buddhism issues no absolute decrees on questions of ethics, leaving individuals free to make their own decisions, so how are we to make a responsible decision? According to Buddhist tenets, the life cycle of a sentient being begins when the consciousness enters the womb, and traditionally this has been considered the moment of conception. Therefore, there is no objection to contraception which interferes with conception without damaging sentient life. Termination of pregnancy, on the other hand, necessarily occurs after conception, so it is not advised.

Buddhist scriptures of various traditions describe the experience of pregnancy from perspectives of both the mother and child. Tibetan texts, moreover, present vivid and remarkably accurate descriptions of the embryo at progressive stages of development in the mother's womb, descriptions that tally with medical science. The texts affirm the preciousness of the human opportunity, yet make no mention of legal rights for the fetus or abortion in cases of rape, incest, severe deformity, or mental, physical, or emotional abuse. However, the Fourteenth Dalai Lama offers the opinion that, "There might be situations in which, if the child will be so severely handicapped that it will undergo great suffering, abortion is permissible. In general, however, abortion is the taking of life and is not appropriate. The main factor is motivation."[1]

Buddhists of old generally recognized and followed the natural course of events. Birth, sickness, old age, and death are natural and inevitable for all sentient beings. New technologies are raising new questions, however, and many Buddhist tenets are being reexamined in light of recent social and scientific developments.

Buddhists also recognize the qualities of love and compassion as important guidelines for living. An abiding interest in the welfare of sentient beings is a feature of even the earliest Buddhist texts. Since phenomena are interdependently related, one's own benefit and harm are closely linked with the benefit and harm of other beings. Without caring and compassion, most importantly the care that mothers give to their children, human beings literally could not survive.

Recognizing that all beings are interrelated and no one wants to suffer, Buddhist social ethics rests on creating maximum mutual benefit for all living beings. These two objectives—the psychological welfare of the individual and the collective welfare of society—are intimately intertwined. This gives rise to an ethic of compassion. The interrelatedness of all phenomena has profound implications, not only for relationships between human beings, but also for human beings' relationships with their natural environment.

Linking the teachings on dependent arising with loving kindness forges a sense of stewardship toward all sentient life. Love and compassion, the antidotes to anger and harmfulness, are cultivated in meditation and then applied to daily living. We generate the wish, "May all beings be happy! May all beings be free from suffering!" and then work to bring it about. The idea is not only to refrain from harming self or others, but to actively assist beings on all levels, including the material, the psychological, and especially, the spiritual.

The world and its cultures would be poorer without this self-less ideal, taught by Christ and Buddha alike. This ideal is embodied in the lives of selfless and compassionate people who work quietly and humbly for the good of the world. It is this compassionate concern for the welfare of others, what the Dalai Lama refers to as "a sense of universal responsibility," that is humanity's greatest asset and its greatest hope.

Chapter 11
The Bodhisattva Peace Training

by Tsering Everest

Whenever we listen to the teachings, practice the teachings, or meditate together with a group of people, obstacles always arise. In Tibetan Buddhism, these obstacles are shown in quite ominous forms: as gigantic, really formidable fellows with bulging eyes and fangs that come to prevent you from meditating. But actually obstacles are a little bit less romantic than that—more like sleep or distractions that cause you to miss a point in the teaching so that you can't consider it in contemplation. If you are distracted by an airplane or a child crying in the back of the room, for example, that makes it very difficult to contemplate and come to an understanding about that point, so how can you meditate upon it? Something that is missed is an obstacle.

The teachings of the path are about human principles or good qualities. The delusions of our minds are tremendously complex. It takes quite a sophisticated approach to untangle the webs of confusion that overlay our minds.

The Tara prayer, which we recite often in the Tibetan tradition, recognizes our inherent perfection, the true nature of all living beings. When we pray to Tara, imagining her as something outside ourselves, the point is to become intimate with perfection. Tara represents the principle of pervasive love, pervasive compassion, the all-powerful principle of benefiting all beings without distinction. We pray to Tara to remove all obstacles to listening to the teachings, obstacles to contemplating them, obstacles to meditating on them, so that the fruit of these teachings may be realized by ourselves and all beings. We pray that these beings not only find immediate happiness, but also ultimate happiness.

Wisdom is without boundaries, so if you have another object of prayer, another wisdom principle that you pray to, that's fine. Absolute truth is essentially the same, whatever name or label we give it. It is like the sky here. We may refer to the Santa Barbara sky, the California sky, or be even more broad-minded and speak of the western hemisphere sky, but in truth, the sky has no fences, no boundaries, and no limits. Similarly, truth is truth, though it manifests in different ways to benefit beings. Various holy beings appear in our world and in our visions. We may have a true sense of unity with perfection in the form of a deity. Truth appears in many manifestations, and for us to cultivate a relationship with any of them is very advantageous.

Sometimes people think that when we pray to Tara, to Buddha, to God, or whomever, the deity looks upon us and thinks, "Oh, what a nice little person," and grants our wishes; if we don't pray, we won't find a parking spot. But if Tara or Buddha or God were like that, none of them would be worthy of our prayers. The principle of enlightened being is completely infinite and compassionate like the sun which shines without discrimination. Whether we pray or not doesn't make any difference in the mind of Tara or Buddha or God. Their qualities are pervasive as the sun's. The difference is that if we live in a deep hole in the ground, we won't experience the light and warmth of the sun.

Prayer is what creates a receptivity in ourselves to the principles of truth available for all beings. When we pray, we open ourselves to perfection, to the understanding of something greater, in order to cultivate qualities in ourselves. Buddha is. Truth is. So if you would like, please join along. We begin with a prayer to Guru Padmasambhava, the father of the lineage of Tibetan Buddhism.

Hung. On the northwest border of the country of Urgyen,
In the pollen heart of a lotus,
Marvelous in the perfection of your attainment,
You are known as the lotus-born
And are surrounded by your circle of many sky dancers.
By following in your footsteps
I pray that you will come to confer your blessings.
Guru Padma Siddhi Hung.

In the space in front of me
The mother of all the victorious ones,
Arya Tara, actually appears and to her I pray.
Now, as I and countless others
Are locked in the ocean of samsaric suffering,
I seek Buddhahood to gain temporary and ultimate happiness
For myself and all living beings.
For this reason, I take refuge in Arya Tara,
The mother of the Pure Realm,
Inseparable from all perfect qualities
Of Buddha, Dharma, Sangha, lama, yidam, and dakini.
From the depth of my heart, I pray,
Evoking from Tara's forehead, throat and heart,
A brilliant surge of rainbow light.
As the light rays touch me and all other beings
The poisonous roots of negative karma,
Sickness, demonic afflictions, and obstacles
Evaporate like dew in the morning sun.
Merit, wisdom, glory, wealth, and longevity
Increase beyond measure.
Illustrious Tara, please be aware of me,
Remove my obstacles
And quickly grant my excellent aspirations.

The bodhisattva peace training is a way of engendering compassion, equanimity, love, and joy in our hearts. It is not meant only for Buddhists. It was conceived as a way of helping people to understand the causes of peace. There are conditions that prevent peace and these need to be overcome. Even people who want nothing to do with the Buddha's teachings are interested in peace. Even people who advocate war have within them a strong longing for peace.

The process begins internally, which is not to say that we shouldn't work toward peace externally as well. The way of training is that after every period of instruction, there is time for contemplation, then a chance to explain and share with others what we have understood. That is why it is called "training."

Sometimes people have the idea that Buddhism means a certain kind of apathy or disdain for worldly involvement—that everything is karma anyway, so we just sit on our cushions. But that point of view is a bit suspect. Does a practitioner serenely meditating in the park ignore a person molesting a child in the woods nearby? Certainly not. We do whatever we can to help other beings. The bodhisattva peace training teaches us to help with love and compassion for both the victim and the aggressor.

The first quality to be developed is compassion. Compassion basically means wishing that others' sufferings would cease. In our world, it is very easy to have compassion for our loved ones, our friends, our neighbors. Sometimes it is even easy for us to have compassion for strangers because we don't have anything against them yet. But it is really difficult to have compassion for those who harm us or harm our loved ones. We can have compassion for our friends and families, but what about the enemy, the war maker, the environmental hazard creator? How do we cultivate compassion for bullies? This is really the point of the bodhisattva peace training.

Our world is in peril. We don't need to be reminded of it. We know very directly, intimately, that there is strife at every level in our world today—at the environmental level, the political level, the psychological level, and so on. Our world is in a complete state of stress and despair.

Buddhists want to relieve the condition of suffering, outwardly and inwardly. This aspiration is further enhanced by the realization that I am not the only one suffering. Just as I suffer, everyone suffers—some more, some less. Whether beings are visible or invisible, none is exempt from suffering. All of them experience the cycles of birth, sickness, old age, and death, of not being able to get what they want, not being able to prevent what they don't want. Even when we get what we want, we often find that we don't want it. There is always this dilemma in our experience of reality, this incongruity. And our own suffering seems to be the most acute because it is our own. Common sense tells us that suffering is the basic condition of all beings.

The bodhisattva peace training is based on bodhichitta. Bodhichitta is a selfless aspiration to attain enlightenment so that all beings can be free of suffering. This compassionate attitude is based on a firsthand understanding of suffering, with no rose-colored glasses. Whatever happiness we experience is, in reality, short-term. We are very lucky if it lasts a whole day. But even if we are fortunate enough to have happiness our whole life, sooner or later that life ends.

Compassion is really foremost. It is said that if compassion is lacking, Buddhahood is unattainable. It is further said that Buddhahood is only attained through the completely selfless effort to benefit other beings. This is what separates the Buddhas and us. The Buddhas want only the welfare of others, while we sentient beings want to benefit ourselves. That is the fork in the road, and that is what makes all the difference: the one path produces enlightenment, while the other leads to spiraling self-indulgence, delusion, confusion, and misery.

The Buddhist path is based on understanding karma, which means cause and effect. We create actions of body, speech, and mind on some impulse or emotion, through a false assumption of self, not knowing our true Buddha nature. Within that context, attachment, hatred, ignorance, and jealousy poison the mind. Under the influence of those poisons, we create karma. Karma is like putting a seed into the ground. Time passes, and in time, the seed sprouts and a plant grows. The seed in the ground produces a fruit.

The mind is tremendously fertile. It produces great consequences. And we are subject to the fruits of our actions. We eat the fruit. The mind is the source of our reality. With our minds, we create harm and we create benefit.

The foremost premise of Buddhadharma is to not kill, to not harm other beings. The first vow of refuge is not to hurt others. If we don't hurt others, we won't experience hurt. So when faced with somebody who is really irritating, really miserable, really awful, really difficult—just the worst—if we understand that person will bear the fruit of his or her actions, it gives us grounds for compassion. If we see our own mother being really brutal, we see that she doesn't understand the law of cause and effect, but one way or the other, she will experience the results of her action, and we wish she wouldn't. We wish she would not experience that kind of suffering. We develop compassion.

We are all subject to the creations of our own minds. It is like a tiger chasing us in a dream. In the dream, the fear, the anxiety, the terror are real. We experience our very bones crunching in the tiger's mouth. But suddenly, we wake up and realize it was only a dream. It seems very true, very real, but eventually we penetrate and understand that it is all a fabrication, a projection of our mind—completely. It is not just the projections I put on my husband or the projections I lay on the parking meter lady. It is the understanding that all of this, totally, from the birds to the trees to the earth to the seas—everything is a projection of our mind, overlaid in confusion.

Some people dream that they are humans. Some people dream that they are animals. Some people dream that they are hell beings. And some people dream that they are starving ghosts. Some people dream that they are very, very powerful, elite, worldly, god-like beings. Nonetheless, all of them are dreaming. All of them experience a variety of sufferings. And it all circulates. Sometimes we dream that we are humans. Sometimes we dream that we are animals. It just goes around and around.

Karma is what produces the dreaming. If one wants to overcome the endless dream existences, one has to overcome karma. Beings have different perceptions of reality according to the level of their confusion. When a mind is more distorted, it experiences the reality of hell. When a mind is less distorted, it experiences the reality of a starving spirit. When the mind is less distorted than that, it experiences an animal existence, and less distorted than that, a human existence, and so on.

In truth, we all have Buddha nature, but in the meantime, what we experience is very real, because in a dream, one is subject to the dream. In this dream, we have to deal with this reality. We've got this world which is about to blow up. We've got this world which is becoming a complete garbage dump. That is the content of our dream, and in this dream, we do the best we can to make conditions better for others. That helps us cultivate the selflessness that is required for attaining enlightenment.

Compassion does not mean idiot compassion. It does not mean letting someone hurt you. It doesn't mean bearing injustice, or allowing oneself to be victimized. It is not compassionate to let others create negative karma, but that doesn't mean we hate our oppressors. We understand that they are deluded beings, trying to gain some benefit for themselves.

The second quality to be developed is equanimity. In the Buddhadharma, there are many meditation methods for helping to cultivate equanimity. One method, taught by the Buddha directly, is that every being—whether human, animal, spirit, friend, or enemy—has been your own mother at some point in the cycle of rebirth. In our society, we don't always have a respectful relationship towards our mother. I don't really know why, but people often harbor a lot of resentment towards their mothers. In Asian cultures, people understand that without a mother, we wouldn't exist as we do now. Whether she has been angry or loving, hurtful or helpful, she gave us a human body, which is an incomparable gift. So there is an appreciation for archetypical motherhood and a respect for the dignity of the mother who has given birth to us.

When we consider that everybody has been our mother, the concept is immense. It is illuminating when we begin seeing the lady at the bank, our children's preschool teacher, our friends, our workers, our employers, and people in other countries as our mother. Everyone we see was once the most important person in our existence. Then we realize that all these beings now only want to be happy, yet they don't quite know how to do it. In fact, they're constantly complicating their conditions—creating worse and worse karmic conditions for themselves by hatred, greed, ignorance, pride, and jealousy. We can also view beings as our children and develop motherly feelings towards them, but more respect is generated if we see them as our parents. Buddhadharma gives us a chance to heal the schism in ourselves concerning our parents. This way we develop compassion and a real aspiration to liberate them from pain and suffering in an ultimate way.

We contemplate all beings with equanimity, whether they harm or help us, whether they are the people in the white hats or the people we cross the street to avoid. In Buddhism, there are no "insignificant others." We realize our interconnectedness with all beings. All of them have at one time or another been our own mother and, in that existence, been very kind to us—giving us a body, nurturing us, feeding us, sharing with us, teaching us to walk and talk. All these blessings of our parents were mixed with a lot of other things that maybe weren't so nice, but still the basic necessities to produce a human existence were all there.

The third quality to be cultivated is love. Many poets have tried to explain what love is, but love, in this case, means wanting others to be happy. To help others requires love, and to love, we have to overcome our own hatred. We want to help the world become peaceful and clean, but if we have anger in our own heart and mind, our anger will hobble us. If we are angry at everybody who pollutes the world or makes war in the world, we become ineffective. Notice that the burn-out rate among environmental and political activists is acutely high. The task is gigantic and anger always gets in the way.

The bodhisattva peace training teaches us that to be effective in the world, we have to begin first within ourselves. Sometimes people don't want to hear this, because what needs to be done out in the world it so crucial, so immediate, so life-threatening. It is absolutely essential that it be done now and that requires that we overcome our hatred now, because if we have hatred, our capacity to help is limited.

For example, my teacher Chakdud Rinpoche was giving a training seminar with a group of feminists working with battered women. It was quite challenging because the level of anxiety and aggression was really acute. Every time Rinpoche would mention the need for compassion, they would vault up to say, "We can't be compassionate. Women are being beaten. Children are being beaten." Finally, Rinpoche said, "All right. Educate the women. Teach the battered women that leaving those violent men is an act of love. The men will no longer have a chance to beat someone, so they won't make negative karma, and if they don't make negative karma, they won't suffer." The solution may be going, it may be staying, but it needs to come from a place of love and compassion.

An act of love is always more powerful than an act of hatred. We need to have compassion towards evil-doers, because for the most part, evil is self-consuming: it destroys the one who creates it. Of course, we do everything we can to help the victim, also. We leap equally with love and compassion to help the victim and the aggressor. Our efforts will reach further when we have complete love and compassion towards everybody.

The fourth quality to be cultivated is rejoicing. Simply put, this means rejoicing that others are happy. Rejoicing means just chiming along—whatever is positive, we join in and rejoice in it, which adds to it. Rejoicing is the antidote to jealousy. And it should be totally genuine—that's the tricky part.

About two years ago, during a bodhisattva peace training, I was in a group that lacked the capacity to have compassion for an aggressor. A Vietnam veteran in the group told a true story about soldiers in a tank division in Vietnam who put explosives into some cookies and threw the cookies to children running after the tank. These men had no intention of staying to see the results of their actions, but as soon as they had thrown the cookies, they got orders to stay in that place. The children who ate the cookies died very terrible deaths. Their mothers came out when the children started screaming, but couldn't figure out what had happened. A man who had been party to this confessed the story to his friend. He had sat many nights with a gun in his mouth because, having done such a thing, life was too difficult for him to bear. Later, though he no longer tried to kill himself daily, he couldn't sit in a room where there was a child or have any relationship with a woman. After the peace training, his friend called to tell him that there are ways to purify the karma of the awful thing he had done and now the man practices Buddhism.

This shows the flaw of trying to judge other people's behavior. Until we attain omniscience, we cannot know another person's suffering. The only suffering we can ever know is our own. From our own suffering, we can guess how intensely others suffer.

Sometimes people think that we should let violence become visible so that we can expose it. But as beginners, we don't yet have that breadth of mind. It takes a great deal of integrity to use forceful or wrathful methods. We're lucky if we can deal with someone who cuts us out of a parking spot in the morning. Our capacities for tolerance and patience are really limited. We have a lot of imperative work to do, and we need strength to continue with the task. Love and compassion don't get tired, weary, and worn out. In America, people have pure intentions and a sincere desire to benefit. They want to make the world a better place, to remedy the conditions of pain and anguish, but they get tired. The bodhisattva peace training is a support for those people who really do want to have a positive impact. To create a positive impact, we have to overcome those traits that cause us to stumble—hatred and negativity. Through the practice, we gain a little more lag time before the knee-jerk reaction to something that ticks us off.

Rinpoche uses a classic example that is my absolute favorite. He says that when someone makes you angry, it is as if they shot an arrow at your heart. It doesn't hit you, but lands right at your foot. Then you pick up the arrow and stab yourself with it over and over and over again. That's what happens. Anything in life can be the cause of getting upset, but the choice to be upset or not is our own. Anger is the worst poison of the mind—the grossest, most obvious one. Subtle anger is even worse.

Every difficult incident in life is an indication of our predicament as a whole. Instead of looking at the little niggle-naggle issues—like who took my stapler and hasn't returned it—if we can look at the whole predicament, it is easier to have compassion. It doesn't matter how intellectual we get about anger, when someone wrecks our car, it is hard to handle. That's why it takes contemplation and effort to distance ourselves from situations, and create a little more gap before reacting. We begin noticing our internal reactions of anger, irritation, or discomfort, without giving expression to them. It requires a great deal of skill to acknowledge our anger, simply reporting it as information, without giving in to it. Motivation is the key.

Sometimes we do things to repay someone who did something nice for us. Sometimes we do things because we feel guilty if we don't. All these kinds of motivation need to be examined, because they show we don't understand our true nature. But when every effort becomes dedicated to the enlightenment of beings, working for others becomes the path for sentient beings to become Buddhas. The only way to achieve the ultimate welfare of others is to attain enlightenment. In the meantime, we do everything we can in an everyday way to benefit others. In this, I think women have great fortitude and capacity.

Buddhism is young enough in this country that we haven't yet learned to integrate our practice and the social needs of beings. As yet, there are not so many Buddhists feeding the poor, helping the sick, and providing selfless service where it's needed. In the first place, there aren't that many Buddhists in the West. And then we are so busy figuring out what Buddhism is, we haven't yet gotten around to effecting the lifestyle of selflessness and service that really *is* Buddhism.

I feel a sparkle of potential now as women begin to organize themselves as Buddhists, as all the different traditions begin to take on the task of handing out the cheese. It's not a big deal to hand out the cheese, but to hand out the cheese with pure intention, so that all beings can attain enlightenment—that's extraordinary. Soon, as our practice matures, we will see that everything we do is done to produce enlightenment for all beings: sweeping the floor, making the bed, working in a corporation, or sailing the high seas. Then we will begin the tasks of helping the poor, helping the elderly, helping the children, and you can bet the women will make it happen.

Response: My desire is to not kill any being, but all I have to do is take a step on the earth, and I have killed many, many ants. How is my karma affected by the ants that I kill unknowingly?

Tsering: This is a very good question. As humans, we are in a "catch-22" situation. In samsara, there is already so much perpetual force for negativity, that almost anything we do may have a negative impact on somebody, whether it's the ants in your house or the beings in the air we breathe. We try our best not to harm or kill, but there is always that risk. The point of practice is that while we are alive, during this short lifetime we have—eighty-five or ninety years at most—we try to do more good than harm.

In the Tibetan tradition, it is explained as being like a snowball rolling downhill. If we can close the door of non-virtue—don't kill, don't steal, don't lie, don't harm, don't commit adultery and other non-virtues—we aren't creating any more negative karma. But we still have all the stores of negative karma we created in past lives, like seed in the ground just waiting for a little water and sunlight to ripen as unpleasant experiences now and in our future. That latent karma has to be purified.

The path is twofold: the accumulation of merit and the purification of karma. We purify the negative karma that's already been created by many different methods, and don't create any more. And we accumulate merit—meaning we do good works—which creates positive, conducive conditions on the path to enlightenment. There are many hazards and pitfalls on the way to enlightenment because of the karma we have created. The more we are able to purify our karma and accumulate merit, the smoother the path becomes. There are said to be two purities: the first is the absolute, perfect nature which is the primordial Buddha nature, and the second is the purity that comes from removing delusion and confusion. The second makes the first obvious.

Once someone asked, "I don't kill anymore, so why do I have to make a promise? Why do I have to take a vow?" And Rinpoche said, "Because there's positive power in a vow." For example, if you promise, "I'll never kill a dragon in my life, no matter what," then from the moment you make the promise, you accumulate the virtue of never breaking that promise. Some people are afraid to take the vow, because they might break it tomorrow, but Rinpoche says that it is better to take it and break it, than not to take it at all. One day of upholding a vow is better than not holding any, because of the positive power of making the commitment.

The bodhisattva peace training usually ends with a ceremony of commitment. Instead of being the one served all the time, we take on the task of serving sentient beings. People may promise to be harmless, to work forever for the sake of all beings, to be humorous, to smile once a day—whatever they are able to do. Whether it is something big or small, they become committed to transformation, and put their word of truth behind it. They express a conviction to work towards peace.

We often find excuses for how we live our lives. We justify ourselves all the time and take ourselves and everything else so seriously. Buddhist practice is to understand that there is no inherent truth to the "I" and "other." From this comes great love, great compassion, and a great openness of mind. The texts give the example of a dream. If you're dreaming and don't know you're dreaming, you experience pain and pleasure, past, present, and future. It's serious and has serious consequences. But as soon as you know it's a dream, that makes a big change—not a little intellectual difference, but a major reality change. If you know the tiger in a dream is a dream, it can't hurt you.

Life is like a dream. The difference is that it takes awareness to understand that this is a dream. The ones who understand this are the siddhas—the ones who can fly, walk on water, and put their handprints in stone. Because we are still bound by samsara, rocks are really solid for us. We are solid in our self-identity and others are solid in their self-identity. When we become free from samsara, we understand that it is all like an illusion, a mirage, a water bubble, a hallucination, or a fantasy. But now, because of our very solid habits, we're stuck. If we can stop taking ourselves so seriously and stop taking things so personally, it will be a relief emotionally and we will have a better basis for practice.

There is a wonderful story about a man who heard that a great teacher was coming to town. He came down out of the high mountains to take instructions. The teacher told him to go back into the mountains and meditate every day from way before dawn to way after midnight, to sleep only three hours a day and eat only a tiny bit of food...just meditate, meditate, meditate. So he did. He went back into the mountains, went to bed way after midnight, got up way before dawn, and ate just a tiny little bit. Thirty years went by like this.

One day he heard that his teacher had come back to town, so he came down out of the mountains and told him, "Honorable Sir, I have been following your instructions perfectly." The teacher asked, "What instructions?" The man said, "You told me to get up before four every morning, go to bed after midnight, eat only a teeny little bit, and meditate, meditate, meditate all day long." The teacher said, "Oh, no, I told you all wrong. I made a mistake. Just forget it," and wouldn't even talk to him anymore. The man was dumbfounded. Still, he had lived on the mountain for thirty years, so he went back to the mountain. He was used to going to bed after midnight, getting up before four, and meditating all day, so he went to bed after midnight, got up at four, did his meditation—and instantly attained enlightenment.

The point is that we do have to go through the effort of transforming ourselves, especially our motivation. All the efforts of practice are like putting a rock in a tumbler and shaking it around. Our essence is perfect, but it's like a crystal dropped in the mud. After a long time, the mud cakes on and becomes like rock. Pretty soon you can't even tell it's a crystal anymore. That's us—lumps of crystal, but the confusion is so thick, nobody can see it. And so we do Dharma practice—prostration, mantras, meditation, striving this way and that, like putting the dirty rock in the tumbler until we get the grit off. After some time, the rough crude covering is all rubbed off and the pure essence is exposed. Our Buddha nature is completely perfect. It isn't diminished by the confusion surrounding it. All we have to do is rub off the rough stuff so that it becomes clear and obvious. Eventually we recognize what we are in essence.

Samsaric delusion is like having serious amnesia. We can't remember if we're a queen, or a pauper, a dog or a cat, but once the amnesia wears off, it's obvious who we are. Dropping away our false identity is the point of practice. We're not creating anything. If we create something, that will also have to drop away eventually, so we're just making more work for ourselves. Meditation is just letting it all drop away naturally.

Response: How is the ego involved?

Tsering: The ego makes the effort. At first we use the mind to change negative self-effort into positive self-effort. That's the first step. Some people have extraordinary capacities. As soon as you tell them the nature of truth, they become enlightened. But most of us have many habitual tendencies and preconceptions that we value and uphold. So first we have to change these negative tendencies, like harming and hating, into positive tendencies, like patience and love. Wisdom is a non-dualistic accomplishment, but in the meantime, we work with the mind to transform negative mind states to positive mind states. We created all this havoc, so now we're cycling round and round in the pain and anguish of samsara. We need to change our negative attitudes to positive ones until the wisdom of ultimate truth becomes obvious.

Response: I would like you to tell us, in one sentence for my simple beginner's mind, how to contemplate these things.

Tsering: First, contemplate the basic predicament of beings: their aspirations for happiness and their dilemma in not being able to find permanent happiness. Second, contemplate that this condition is not unique to one being or another, but is a condition that afflicts all of us throughout all our existences. Third, cultivate a sincere wish that suffering will end. Fourth, understand the equality of all beings in their absolute nature and the suffering of being disassociated from that nature. Generate love and compassion for all beings equally, both victims and aggressors. Rejoice in their finding ultimate happiness and complete fulfillment. Finally, contemplate "How can I make a difference?" and make a commitment to work for the fulfillment of all beings.

Now, let us dedicate the merit, the benefits of whatever transformation has occurred, to the welfare of all beings. In Buddhist practice, we first generate the intention: Why do we meditate? Why do we listen to the teachings? Why do we practice? Then there is the actual practice itself. And then there is the selfless dedication of all merit of the practice to the welfare of beings, like a gift of the merit we created now, as well as all past and future merit. We amass it all together by our pure heart and pure intention, tie it with a bow, and give it for the sake of beings, with a prayer:

> May all beings find happiness and the causes of happiness.
> May they be free from suffering and the causes of suffering.
> May they find the ultimate happiness of enlightenment
> For the peoples and the nations of the earth.
> May not even the names disease, famine, war, and suffering be
>   heard,
> But rather may their moral conduct, wealth, and prosperity be
>   increased,
> And may supreme good fortune and well-being always arise.

Chapter 12

The Monastic Experience

Karma Lekshe Tsomo

Soon after the Buddha became enlightened under the Bodhi tree, some of his friends decided to practice as he did and said that they wanted to become monks. The Tibetan histories say that as soon as he spoke the words, "Come here," their heads spontaneously became shaved and they were clothed, miraculously, in orange robes. The first five monks, his first disciples, had been close spiritual friends who accompanied him as he searched for a valid path to enlightenment. After these five, many thousands of others joined the order, first men and, some years later, women.

In the early days of the Buddha's teaching, there were no precepts and no particular regulations. Some time later, however, it happened that one of the monks went home to his wife. The laypeople questioned his behavior and came to the Buddha saying, "Look at this monk! He went home and slept with his wife!" And the Buddha said, "This is not appropriate conduct for a monk. A monk should not engage in sexual activities. Henceforth all monks should refrain from sexual activity."[1] This became the first precept for the monks and, later, for the nuns. From then on, whenever a question of appropriate conduct arose, it was put before the Buddha. Incidents of inappropriate conduct served as precedents from which regulations were formulated. These regulations, or precepts, served as guidelines for the training of the monks and nuns. The precepts, then, are guidelines for helping regulate one's actions of body, speech, and mind in a way that will be conducive for spiritual development. Eventually there were over two hundred precepts for the monks.

The question of celibacy was a key issue. Of course, the Buddha did not expect everyone to become monks and nuns. Buddhist practice is open to everyone, whether they are celibate or not. But, from the beginning, the Buddha recommended celibacy for those who wished to engage in intensive spiritual practice, and this is the lifestyle adopted by Buddhist monks and nuns. Initially, they wandered as mendicants from place to place and stayed in retreat together during the rainy season to avoid treading on insects as they went out to gather alms. Gradually, settled monastic communities evolved.

Five years after the establishment of the order of monks, the Buddha's stepmother (who was also his aunt) asked to join the order. The Buddha hesitated, as it was not customary for women in that society to leave their homes, and the mendicant lifestyle was rigorous even for men. To allow women to live a wandering lifestyle, traveling here and there and living on alms, was a radical innovation and quite threatening to the whole social structure. However, the Buddha did allow its establishment and thus we have the order of bhikshunis, the counterpart of the order of bhikshus, or fully ordained monks. In addition to the more than two hundred precepts that had been created as a result of certain monks' misbehavior, another hundred or more precepts were created as a result of certain nuns' misbehavior, so today we bhikshunis hold over three hundred precepts. In the Chinese Dharmagupta lineage, which is the only living lineage of full ordination for women in Buddhism today, we have 348 precepts.

Living a monastic lifestyle has been very helpful to me. From the Buddhist viewpoint, spirituality, or Dharma, is that which leads us out of samsara, the cycle of birth and death. Desire, aversion, and ignorance are the primal forces that keep us revolving around and around. At the moment of death, it is due to desire that the untrained consciousness enters another body. So to free ourselves from the sufferings of cyclic existence, it is essential to cut through desire. In this way, being celibate is helpful on the path—not essential, not required for everyone, but helpful.

Monasticism doesn't necessarily mean solitude. To be a nun or a monk doesn't mean that we sit in a cave and gather dust. Although nuns and monks may train in a secluded environment, they usually serve the community in various capacities. They contribute to society as teachers, counselors, spiritual friends, preceptors, ritual specialists performing funerals and blessings, and in many other ways. Thus nuns and monks do participate actively in everyday life. Renunciation in Buddhism is not something external, like giving up sugar or coffee or chocolate. It is an internal attitude of renouncing the whole tiresome cycle of birth and rebirth.

My path was pretty clear from the beginning, since my family name was Zenn. I was raised a Christian, but kept coming up with questions about life and death that weren't being answered in the churches in Malibu, California. The children at school kept teasing me about being a Zen Buddhist, so I started reading books on Zen when I was thirteen, and the minute I opened them, it all rang true. I thought, "This is it!" My mother says I announced that I was a Buddhist when I was eleven.

Of course, it wasn't easy learning about Buddhism in the fifties. There were very few Buddhist teachers in America and no Buddhist centers. There weren't even many books available besides the fantastic tales of Lobsang Rampa, but I read everything I could get my hands on. When I was nineteen I went to Japan to go surfing, and in the winter when it got too cold to surf, I went to a monastery and started meditating. After a year in Japan, I travelled through Southeast Asia, India, Nepal, and a lot of other countries. I visited many temples, chanted the "Om mani padme hum" mantra of the Tibetan tradition, and wrote the *Heart Sutra* over and over again in Chinese, but still there were no opportunities for actually studying Buddhism. Even by the sixties things weren't set up yet for Westerners to study Buddhism in Asia. Eventually I went back to the United States and did degrees at Berkeley and the University of Hawaii.

In 1972, I heard that His Holiness the Dalai Lama had established the Library of Tibetan Works and Archives to help preserve Tibetan culture and also to teach Buddhism to Western people, so I went to Dharamsala in northern India. Geshe Ngawang Dhargyey, a well-known monk-scholar, was teaching, and since there was translation into English, it was a perfect opportunity. I studied with other great Tibetan meditation masters, such as Kalu Rinpoche, and went all over India for intensive vipassana meditation retreats with U. S. N. Goenka of the Burmese tradition. The more I got into Dharma, the more I loved it. Eventually I decided I'd like to practice full-time, so I realized a recurring dream and became a nun in 1977.

Of course, in Buddhism there is no obligation to become a nun. Living a celibate lifestyle is just one option, but for me it seemed ideal. I took the novice ordination with Gyalwa Karmapa in France in 1977, and since there was no tradition of full ordination for women in the Tibetan tradition, I went to Korea and became fully ordained there in 1982. I went through the ordination process again in Taiwan and trained in a monastery there for six months. After that, I went back to Dharamsala and studied for six years at the Institute of Buddhist Dialectics, a non-sectarian study center following the traditional Tibetan monastic curriculum. This curriculum includes a twelve-year study of Buddhist logic, debate, psychology, philosophy, and monastic discipline.

While living in Dharamsala, I helped found a small monastic study center for women of the Tibetan tradition just five minutes from the temple of His Holiness. It is called Jamyang Chöling Institute for Buddhist Women and now has five branches in remote regions of the Himalayas, with over 150 nuns altogether. Every day we do meditation and chanting together, as well as continue an intensive program of study and philosophical debate. Jamyang Choling is non-sectarian, vegetarian, and aims at training women of various ethnic backgrounds as teachers of Dharma.

So many nuns wanted to join the program that we had no more living space, so I went looking for a piece of land in the countryside nearby. While walking under some low-hanging branches, a snake apparently fell from a tree and bit me, but since I didn't realize it at once, it was eight days before I got to a hospital for treatment. By that time gangrene had set in and the venom had seriously damaged my arm. Somehow I survived the bite and, even more miraculously, survived three months in Indian and Mexican hospitals. The experience taught me many things, especially about impermanence, suffering, patience, compassion, and the interdependence of living beings.

Although I cherish solitude, there are many benefits to living in a contemplative community. For one, I am lazy by nature, so it is very useful to be in a disciplined monastic environment where time is not wasted in worldly pursuits. I enjoy meditating with a group. The structure of a monastery is supportive; the atmosphere is intensified and blessed with the practice of many others.

Living in a community also means that duties such as food preparation and cleaning can be shared, which saves a lot of time that can be used for study and meditation. Even while working, there is the presence of other meditators to inspire one's mindfulness. There are fewer distractions, since there are no parties or entertainments, and presumably there are fewer conflicts, too, since all members of the community have similar goals and lifestyles. I find that monastic communities for women, in particular, have a special quality.

In an ideal community, there are also role models who serve as guides and provide inspiration either through their advice or simply by their presence. Spiritual cultivation requires proper conditions for maximum personal growth. At least in the beginning, it is helpful to avoid activities that distract us from the path. After five or ten years of training under the guidance of a qualified master, it may be possible to continue the practice on one's own. Of course, it is not necessary to live in a monastery to practice Dharma; for some it may even be harmful. But for those so inclined, monastic life can be very conducive to spiritual growth. I think that life in contemplative Buddhist communities should be available as an alternative for women, providing an alternative to the often hectic, often meaningless life in the modern world.

Eko Susan Noble

I did my training and was ordained at Mt. Koya, the headquarters of the Shingon sect, located in the mountains thirty-five miles south of Osaka in central Japan. Mt. Koya is considered a sacred mountain and, according to Japanese custom, for well over a thousand years women were not allowed to go to the top of the mountain. Consequently, the order of nuns in this tradition is relatively recent. Full ordination in the "men's" lineage was officially instituted in 1872, although there have been lay women practitioners of high realization in the tradition for centuries.

During the past one hundred years or so, women have had the opportunity to ordain in the lineage officially and train at Mt. Koya. The precepts we hold are exactly the same as those of our male colleagues. The words "monk" and "nun" are still used in Japan, in our ordination certificates, for example, but I usually refer to myself as a priest, because the word "nun" in English implies taking a vow of celibacy, and that is not generally the case for Buddhist clergy in Japan.

The Nuns' Training Institute at Mt. Koya was established in 1978 and a new training temple was built in 1987. Prior to that time, women would train by themselves, under their master's direction, in one of the 123 other temples at Mt. Koya. For a short period of time, they did train together with the men in the Men's Training Institute, which has a much longer history as an institution. Now there is a beautiful facility with space for sixteen women to train each year.

Foreigners in Japan who want to study Buddhism are usually directed to Zen temples which accommodate their special needs. It is possible to sustain an intense practice at a Zen monastery without mastering Japanese. In the Shingon tradition, however, one is required to read texts in both Chinese and Sanskrit. Although Western men have trained privately, I am the first Western woman ever to be ordained in the Shingon tradition and the first foreigner ever to enter either the men's or the women's training temples at Mt. Koya. There was a lot of media attention when I began my studies and this was, at times, very difficult for me. Now I am quite grateful because a documentary was produced that shows our traditional training in the Shingon tradition and provides a good introduction for others who may be interested.

Mt. Koya has a physical beauty that is quite unique. There is a special vibration on the mountain, as it is one of the power places in Japan. In the East Asian Buddhist traditions, sacred mountains with these special energies and magnetic fields were often chosen as places for spiritual practice. I was told that airplanes don't fly over Mt. Koya because the energy radiating from it interferes with radar systems. I felt very privileged to be allowed to do my training there, although as a test case, so to speak, I found myself under some pressure. I had to promise not to ask for any relaxation of the rules just because I was not Japanese. Given the cultural differences and linguistic difficulties I faced, this was a great challenge, but becoming a priest in the Shingon tradition was what I wanted to do more than anything else. The experience was precious yet very difficult in many respects.

One might have romantic visions of life in a beautiful temple on top of a sacred mountain, but the real spiritual worth was in the dynamic relationship of living very closely with fifteen other women. The head nun was both a bodhisattva and a drill sergeant. Monastic training in Japan now follows an academic schedule, with three terms in the course of a year's study.

Shingon training traditionally begins with a basic novice ordination in which we shave our heads, receive the robes, and take ten precepts. The first and third terms were devoted to learning basic rituals, chanting sutras each morning and evening, and doing a very intensive academic course of study. We learned how to wear the robes, sit, chant, and live according to Japanese monastic standards. Our academic course work consisted of nineteen classes, six days a week, eight hours a day: classes in history of the Buddhist traditions, traditional chanting of Sanskrit hymns, precepts, monastic discipline, Sino-Japanese and Sanskrit calligraphies. In addition, we studied social welfare, how to teach the Dharma, tea ceremony, flower arrangement, and religious dance. It was a very well-rounded course of study designed to introduce us to all aspects of what will be a lifetime's study in various disciplines.

There was a constant pressure to be very, very mindful in all aspects of our lives. I could tell many funny stories about the mistakes we made, which seem very minor but become big issues in a closed community. This was the first time that I, an American, was not able to speak my mind and it was very good practice. It soon became clear that the welfare of the community was the primary concern and the expression of my personal opinion was not necessarily essential for our practice and life together.

The second term was when we did the traditional ascetic training in ritual meditation called the Fourfold Preparatory Enlightenment Practice. This is the Shingon barrier gate: one hundred days

of extremely intensive ritual sadhana practices. Successful completion of these practices is required to receive transmission of the
Dharma lineage, the first level of empowerment, and full ordination as a priest. Other higher levels of empowerment come after
years of further training and experience in the practice.

The Fourfold Preparatory Enlightenment Practice is designed
to be very challenging. It is a process of purification, as well as a
determination of whether one has a deep karmic affinity with the
Shingon tradition. Long hours of meditation bring up memories
of all the inappropriate actions committed in this lifetime, and one
atones for them. Very profound changes take place as relationships
to the different Buddhist deities are established.

We rose at 2:00 A.M. and performed sadhana practices for twelve
to fifteen hours each day. Sitting Japanese-style on one's heels (*seiza*)
on a hard wooden surface covered only by a thin bamboo mat was
physically difficult even for my Japanese classmates. Developing
concentration in the rituals and meditation required in the sadhanas
was a great mental challenge. Then there is the internal drama and
questioning: "Am I going to make it or not?" Out of sixteen women
who began the training, eleven of us graduated.

Most of the women were either single or widowed. There was
one other woman who was married, as I was at the time. Both our
husbands were Shingon priests. I remember my other married class-
mate clearly because she was the best novice of all, both academi-
cally and personally. Just two weeks before the final Transmission
of the Dharma lineage, we received news that her husband, in
trying to take care of their two young children, had fallen ill, so
she chose to return to help her family. This seemed to us all a true
bodhisattva act, giving up her personal desire of receiving the
ordination. Her heart had truly opened as a result of spiritual
practice.

As part of our training, we also did the traditional seven-hun-
dred-mile pilgrimage to eighty-eight temples on the island of
Shikoku. It takes about two months to walk the route, but we trav-
eled by bus with a group of laypeople from all over Japan. It was
very moving, because many of our fellow pilgrims were elderly
and were fulfilling a lifelong dream by doing this pilgrimage. They
were in tears at the end. I found their faith and sincerity a very

inspiring and memorable part of my training. Deep karmic connections brought me, an American, together with a very disparate group of Japanese women. This was an educational experience for me as well as for them. It challenged all our preconceptions, making us look at things in a different way.

It is an open secret that it was actually women who first brought Buddhism to Japan. Around 552 C.E. three women of Korean ancestry went from Japan to the Korean peninsula, were ordained, and returned to found the first Buddhist temple in Japan, under the patronage of a noble family. This fact is not often mentioned in the histories of Japanese Buddhism which have been written by male scholars. Traditionally, Japan could be considered a matrilineal culture with the imperial line descending from the sun goddess Amaterasu Omikami. Patriarchy was instituted with Confucian influence from China and this accounts for the change in historical perspective.

As Buddhism was transmitted from India, moving northward into China, Korea, and then to Japan, different conceptions arose concerning the observance of precepts. Even in India, shortly before his death, the Buddha made a statement that some of the minor precepts could be changed, and certainly in Japan there have been some very radical changes.

The major departure in the Japanese development regarding precepts was first initiated by the Tendai master Saicho. Saicho wrote voluminously on the precepts and felt that adherence to the full 250 precepts codified in India was inappropriate for the Japanese people. His arguments and rationale, in line with both the final statement of the Buddha and the cultural ethos of Japan, led to the prominence of the bodhisattva precepts as codified in the Heian period (781-1191) in the Tendai and Shingon traditions. Some of the impetus behind this movement was to re-establish the spiritual importance of the precepts, since the Heian government had begun to control the number of priests ordained in Japan and the entire system had become tainted by political and aristocratic influence.

Both Saicho and Kukai, the founder of the Shingon tradition, were ordained at the government ordination platform in Nara and took the standard 250 precepts as they were transmitted from

China. Gradually, the standard precepts observed came to be the ten bodhisattva precepts, while in the Shingon tradition, tantric precepts were also observed.

In 1224, Shinran, the founding master of the Jodo Shinshu (True Pure Land) tradition, developed what was essentially a lay priesthood. He felt that there should be no separation between the priesthood and the laity, that this was a great hindrance to the transmission of the Dharma. He openly married a woman who had been a Buddhist nun, which was quite a revolutionary action. Thus began the tradition of the married priesthood. Up until that time, even though the monks and nuns were primarily observing the bodhisattva precepts, they were usually celibate and led monastic lives. In later historical developments, virtually all of the Buddhist schools in Japan stopped observing celibacy. Often the Japanese way of observing the precepts has been in conflict with other Buddhist traditions, because it is such a radical departure from the tradition observed in India.

When the *shoguns* ruled Japan during the Tokugawa period (1600-1867), Buddhist temples essentially became arms of the military government. Buddhist priests, instead of being allowed to preach the Dharma and minister to people freely, became government bureaucrats, taking care of birth, death, and marriage records. The government at that time divided each town evenly into different parishes to minimize the influence of any one particular Buddhist denomination. People were forced to become parishioners of a particular temple, not by personal belief but by the geographical location of the family home. It was an expedient move by the government to both control and institutionalize the support of the temples, in that each family was required to give to the nearest one. The temple priest, in turn, kept a very good eye on everybody's activities and reported directly to the government authorities.

When the Tokugawa period ended and Emperor Meiji was restored to the throne, a system of State Shinto was introduced. This began a period of forced separation of Buddhist temples and Shinto shrines, which had grown together in such away that no conflict was seen between the native animistic tradition and Buddhism. The forces of nature, deified in Shinto as *kami*, were identified as manifestations of the Buddhas.

After a period of strict separation of temples and shrines, there was a period of persecution of Buddhism in Japan. A conscription ordinance issued in 1872 by Emperor Meiji permitted Buddhist priests to eat meat, to marry officially, to grow their hair, and to take a family name, and legally ended the practice of going for alms (*takuhatsu*). There were over half a million clerics—Buddhist priests and nuns—in Japan in 1865. Five years later that number had been reduced to 77,000. Temples were closed or razed and very important aspects of spiritual practice were changed. This relaxing of the rules was actually a very clever way of breaking the strength of the monastic system. Vast numbers of monks and nuns could not be accommodated in the remaining temples, so most of them returned to lay life. When the persecution began to let up, some temples were re-opened. The priests, rather than abandon their wives and children, brought them back to the temples, having discovered that "enlightenment is enlightenment," with or without a family. They adapted in a very creative way, setting the tone for Buddhist observance in modern Japan.

The majority of temples in Japan have essentially become hereditary, passed down to the oldest son or daughter. Over half of my classmates were there because of a strong vocation, rather than because of family duty, a much higher percentage than in the men's school. This affected their attitude toward the practice.

The Japanese have quite flexible attitudes about the issue of celibacy. The fact that more women than men priests observe celibacy has to do with the cultural expectations. It is easy for a man who is a priest to have his wife support his activities and help him fulfill that role, whereas for a woman to be a priest and be married in Japan is almost an impossibility. It is problematic for her to fulfill both roles, given what is normally expected of a "wife" in that culture, and there is little support for doing so. Most of the celibate female priests I have met find a way of maintaining their freedom. I was told that I could make my own decision, depending on what best suits my own personal situation and benefits my practice.

Here we get down to the issue of creating a situation that is most beneficial for practice. How can we make the most progress? Traditionally, whether married or not, one is expected to be celibate during the training at Mount Koya. Also, when we do certain ritual practices, we find it necessary to preserve the energies in the body and to cultivate them in certain ways. Because Shingon is a tradition of Vajrayana, or Tantric Buddhism, the success of our yogic practices is in balancing the body's energies. From this perspective, during times of intensive specialized practice, maintaining celibacy is essential to the very subtle and delicate opening of different centers in the body and to the cultivation of those energies.

Furyu Schroeder

I'm from the "California school" of Zen. I began training at the San Francisco Zen Center about fifteen years ago. Our temple was founded by Shunryu Suzuki Roshi, a Japanese Zen master who came to America in the 1950s. By the time I arrived, Suzuki Roshi had already died and Richard Baker Roshi was the Abbot. In the community at that time there was a tremendous feeling of growth and vitality with many young and sincere students devoting their life energy to creating a Buddhist Sangha out of the bedrock of the 1960s hippie culture.

The Zen Center's city property is located in a black ghetto, and I understand that Suzuki Roshi intentionally placed it there, not wanting us to be off in some safe space, avoiding difficulties. I lived there for five years and worked in two of the Zen Center businesses, first the Tassajara Bread Bakery and then at Greens Restaurant.

When I first arrived in the community, I had no idea what it meant to "practice for the benefit of others," but I was enthusiastic about joining whatever was happening. In those days that was quite a lot. We'd get up every morning at 4:00 A.M. to sit *zazen*, chant morning service, and clean the temple. Then we'd catch a bus to the bakery and begin an eight-hour day of selling hot muffins, fresh bread, pastries, and pots of coffee. At the end of the day my young co-workers and I would often take in a movie or go out to dance. When you're twenty, you can do that, with energy to spare. And it made me very happy to have such a rich mixture of activities and textures in each day.

I soon realized, however, that Zen Center expected all of us to enter the monastery at some time if we wanted to remain within the community. The monastery was Tassajara, which is located at the remote end of a long country road in the middle of the Los Padres National Forest. Tassajara had a reputation for strictness. There were many young somber-looking men and women there, some with shaved heads, giving the place a Marine boot camp look, so I kept putting off the inevitable. Finally my time ran out and I found myself packed and off to camp. I remember my last night at the City Center sitting at dinner with Reb Anderson, now one of the Zen Center abbots, who said to me, "Good luck, cadet!"

Traditionally in Japan monks spend time sitting outside the monastery gate before being admitted, to demonstrate their sincerity. This waiting period is called *tangaryo*. At the time I went to Tassajara, it could last from five to fourteen days, depending on how well we were sitting. For years I had been afraid of *tangaryo*, so it was a surprising relief to actually be doing it. What I remember from this experience was the length of a day—the timeless transformation of sensations, sounds, and sunlight. Sure enough, eventually it was over.

At Tassajara the weather is either very nice, very cold, or very hot. We didn't have heat in our rooms, so in winter our bodies were the source of heat. The warmth I got from the food I'd eaten, from the hot baths or the stove, gave warmth through the night in my sleeping bag. I've come to believe that renunciation reveals the primal forces in human life, not simply by doing without luxuries, but by thoroughly embracing all aspects of our body and mind, going deeper than our usual notion of comfort and safety will allow.

During the first year I spent in the monastery, I was still tightly woven into the "outside world," making phone calls, getting and sending lots of letters. But by the second year, the connections started to unweave and then I felt as though I had actually arrived. Everything in my life was right there. At the opening of each ninety-day practice period, we had a special ceremony during which the doors to the outside were shut. At the huge gate that leads to the road, we'd chant the *Heart Sutra* and then slide the big drawbar across the door. No one else would enter Tassajara for the duration of the practice period and those of us inside would get to know each other very well.

Although we weren't formally ordained when we went to Tassajara, we were really living like monks—up early for sitting meditation, studying the ancient texts, sharing the work of caring for the monastery. We would clean the road, rake the leaves, just do what we were told, with nothing to worry about. We lived the simplest life and had this great freedom. One of the main elements of training in a monastic program is following the schedule. As long as I kept following the schedule, I got a tremendous amount done. When I had lots of free time, I didn't get anything done.

We had no money at all. It was the oddest thing to see a dollar bill. In fact, if someone had offered any of us the choice between a dollar bill or a cookie, I'm sure we all would have taken the cookie.

The most basic rules which governed our daily life were the Buddhist precepts: not killing, not stealing from others, not lying or slandering. For me, the precepts were like a recipe for how to cook or how to create a human being. We put all these humans in a big pot together, over time, with low heat. If the heat's too high, they will pop out. Very gradually, we begin to see a transformation—little butterflies start to pop out here and there. It is quite wonderful. My feeling, too, is that it's very useful to internalize monastic life and take the monastery wherever you go. By "monastery," I mean the remembering and expressing the Buddha's way of life, day after day, forever and ever.

Most of the time during the practice periods, we observed "noble silence," with very little talking. But then when summer arrived, everything changed. After months of this rigorous monastic training program, which we did with great sincerity, the summer guest season arrived. It was a tremendous twist. One week we would be in a *sesshin*, standing in the kitchen preparing gruel for the monks' meals, and the next week, all of a sudden, we would hear people giggling down by the coffee machine. The guests had arrived and they were wearing only their bathing suits! Sometimes it was difficult to deal with this intrusion. If we resented it, then we had to work with our resentment.

What I have come to understand from my experience at Tassajara is that my own body is the site or womb of practice. My own mind is the monastery. In order to see this, sometimes it's necessary to close the doors, put the cat out, and quiet down. It is difficult for

most of us to organize our lives to allow for this kind of quiet retreat. Through most of our lives we are completely bound by commitments, obligations, and responsibilities. The opportunity to be
in a place where other people agree to live this simple way is a
great gift. It is a chance to find out about the person we really want
to be, even if we don't know it yet.

I spent two consecutive years at Tassajara, but when I returned
to San Francisco, I couldn't reintegrate. I felt as though I'd gotten
lost between the worlds, so finally I went back and spent another
year at Tassajara. Then I went to Green Gulch, which is a nice middle
ground. It's close to town and there are plenty of people around,
but still the basic monastic form prevails. We sit every morning
and every evening. The internalized monastery is the dominant
thought-form, or tone, at Green Gulch.

About five years ago I took priest ordination and then last year,
for a period of time, I was the *shuso*, or head monk, which was my
second ordination. The head monk does everything that a novice
does, but is also considered a role model for new students. At the
end of a three-month training session, in a formal ceremony, the
head monk is tested by friends and fellow students. During the
ceremony, with a fan in one hand and a staff in the other, you sit
next to the statue of the Buddha facing all your Dharma brothers
and sisters, who start asking you questions one after another. It's
tremendous and terrifying. As I was going in to be questioned, I
asked one of the abbots, "Is there any way out of this?" Pointing to
the hallway where the ceremony was going to take place, he said,
"Yes, right through that door."

Nora Ling-yun Shih

The monastery where I lived for a year, Hsi Lai Temple in Los
Angeles, both belongs to and is faithful to the Chinese tradition.
This tradition began almost two thousand years ago, when Buddhism was brought to China via the Silk Road. The Chinese adopted
the monastic tradition, including an order of nuns.

The monastery sometimes can have as many as four hundred
monks and nuns in residence and sometimes as few as one hundred. There are people from Malaysia, Singapore, Nepal, and sometimes Korea, but most are from Taiwan. The type of practice we do

is the traditional combination of Ch'an (the ancestor of Japanese Zen) and Pure Land. Ch'an is a lonely and very private practice, whereas Chinese Pure Land is the samadhi of sound—a community practice.

At certain times, for special ceremonies, the temple becomes a community center, buzzing with life. People bring not only their aged relatives, some practically on stretchers, but also their children. All the generations come together. The Chinese maintain a very strong connection between daily life and spiritual practice, and so food is usually offered to everyone immediately after the service. The collecting and giving of food, and the attitude of service are very important. Monks and nuns learn to cook and are strictly vegetarian.

The way of the precepts serves as a guide. The five basic precepts are simply a code of behavior for civilized people in society. In the Chinese approach, the eight precepts are for people who are interested in deepening their experience of Buddhist practice. The temple offers the eight-precept ceremony for people to engage in monastic practice for twenty-four hours. The next step is the ten precepts, which is the first ordination for monastics. Later comes the higher ordination, which is the final step in leaving the household life.

Celibacy is not seen as something connected with intimacy—pure or impure, desirable or undesirable, a free choice or anything like that. Essentially celibacy has to do with not having preferences. Without preferences, everyone is as important as everyone else. The precepts, as a code of behavior, are part of the Indian heritage and cannot simply be changed at will. What the Chinese have done is amend the precepts by adding the bodhisattva vows.

During the bodhisattva ordination, the person simply vows to consider compassion first and at all times. The practice of the bodhisattva of compassion is to use the precepts as doors that open towards compassionate mindfulness. We vow to refrain from killing, out of compassion for others who value their lives as dearly as we do. The Mahayana tradition, which has prevailed in China, is based on the bodhisattva's compassionate way of life. In this tradition, it is believed that one of the reasons for being ordained is to serve other beings. In our monastery, we work about fourteen hours a day. Each of us has a job that rotates every three months, so that everyone learns every aspect of operating the monastery.

At the monastery, there are outreach programs, especially Pure Land practice with chanting. Women have every opportunity and are valued equally with men. In fact the first abbot, who was instrumental in building this huge monastic complex, was a woman.

Here in the West, the Buddhist traditions that are transmitted to us are more or less spliced together with Eastern culture. I have some questions about this. It is a wonderful practice, a real challenge, and I appreciate it, but there is a constant pressure. Like taking cod liver oil, it's good for you, but there's another side to it. I have the feeling that we Westerners need to define for ourselves the meaning of Buddhist monasticism and what the training represents. I've practiced many styles—Japanese, Vietnamese, a little bit of Vipassana, and now mainly Chinese Ch'an—and I've found that there is quite a bit of difference between the way Western and Asian women perceive themselves and interact. In my experience, the Asian acceptance of hierarchy is quite different from what many Western women are prepared to handle. I sometimes seriously question whether this is really what the Buddha's teachings are all about.

For me, the question is: How is Buddhist monasticism relevant to life here in the West? Self-discipline is basic to learning how to live with other sentient beings, but sometimes the discipline seems overly stringent. For me, to prove that I am as capable as a man serves no purpose, for a man is not something that I want to be. In the past Buddhism adapted to the cultures of different countries. When we look around, we see that many Western Buddhists are actively involved with ecology, human rights, AIDS patients, and so on, while Asian Buddhists are still involved with the perpetuation of certain traditions. I fully respect both approaches; they are simply different.

I don't mind the stringent discipline. It helps me curb my ego as well as my arrogance. Chinese culture is one of the oldest cultures still around and I respect that. However, many useful Western ideas are not accepted simply because they are not part of the tradition and don't fit the structure. A great deal of the monastic training involves culture, which I find very beautiful. However, that may be one of the reasons why people have difficulty relating to Buddhism. At sesshins, we close the doors, put on black clothes, and sit. When we come out, people ask, "When are these Buddhists going to wake up?"

For example, take the problem of environment. The conservation of both water and trees, along with the very real ethical problems arising from recent social and economic developments, is of great importance. So, as I meditate on the deeds of the bodhisattva, I wonder how things will come together for the Western Sangha. I deeply honor the robes. I was immensely moved when, after a very long time, I was privileged to finally receive them. The Buddha dressed according to the standards and attitudes of his time. Even the color he chose for the robes was intended to make a statement. Thus it is important to consider what is of intrinsic value in the Buddha's teachings and how the teachings address the problems of today, here and now.

Jacqueline Mandell

The first time I saw a nun, an ordained Western woman in India, I thought that I would never ordain. Rather, I would practice as a laywoman. The Dharma is for laypeople, I thought, and there is no longer any reason to practice as a monastic. Yet later, as I began to challenge my own practice, I took whatever steps were necessary to put me face to face with myself. When I came back to the United States from three years in Asia, I started thinking more about ordination. My goal was to be a wandering nun, but normally nuns aren't allowed to do forest retreats. So in 1975, in an act of defiance, I took a Tibetan nomad tent to the National Forest in Sawtooth Mountain and created my own forest retreat. I meditated there until I was visited by a grizzly bear. The experience of practicing alone in the forest was incredibly refreshing to me and whetted my appetite for more.

Around the same time, I met Mahasi Sayadaw. I was invited to ordain at his monastery in Burma (now Myanmar) and given a special visa to do so. I took the eight precepts on January 1, 1980, and was a nun for three months in Rangoon, Burma. This reflects the tradition of temporary ordination available in Burma, a tradition I think is fantastic for Western society.

Buddhist women doing monastic practice in Burma sleep only four hours a day; the other twenty hours are spent in meditation. They take eight precepts: to refrain from lying, stealing, killing, sexual conduct, alcohol and drugs, jewelry and adornments, high and luxurious beds, and food after noon. For a ten-precept nun, one of the eight precepts is divided into two, and then the tenth precept is not to touch money or gold. This last precept makes a very distinct difference, since it entails total renunciation. You can't use money or barter anything.

I wore robes and a nun would shave my head once a week at the monastery. Since I was authorized as a teacher through Mahasi Sayadaw, I was given special treatment and far more food than anyone could eat. Then people would sit and watch me eat.

There is a beautiful sense of selflessness in this. People are not watching *you* meditate or watching *you* eat; they're just very happy to provide support for you to practice. Because I was the first Western woman to ordain at the Thatnana Yeiktha Meditation Center, there were movie cameras and flashbulbs and my whole ordination was documented.

After my stay at the Center, I stayed at various nunneries, some solely for nuns and others associated with monasteries for monks. Certain nunneries had a very strong study program while others required only that the nuns live very, very simply. Thus I had a good opportunity to experience the various ways in which a nun might live. Simplicity is related to renunciation. Renunciation sounds like a pushing away, but actually it is a taking in. It is deeply connected with simplicity and the basics of life, and keeps one very mindful.

Precepts are not imposed. They are something one chooses to keep. The beauty of ordination is that it is a choice. No one says that a Buddhist must ordain. That's why I feel that temporary ordination is a wonderful opportunity. In the book *Feminine Ground*, edited by Jan Willis, the accomplished Tibetan nun Jetsun Lochen Rinpoche is quoted as saying, "Even if they have been nuns for only a week, they will be different forever afterwards."

I also took the ten-precept forest ordination with my teacher, the late Taungpulu Sayadaw, in Boulder Creek, California. My ordination, both as an eight-precept nun and as a ten-precept nun, is a strong force within me even now. Whatever I do, I try to do as simply and concisely as possible.

The nuns in Burma go on weekly alms rounds with large baskets on their heads. Unlike the monks, who gather only cooked food, the nuns usually gather uncooked grains and food offerings which they cook themselves. The order of fully ordained nuns has died out in Burma and some say this occurred because of a lack of support. Burmese nuns wear a different robe than the monks. It has a long-sleeved blouse, wrap-around skirt, a long apron, and an outer robe. The colors range from saffron yellow to beautiful pinks. At my second ordination, which was with Taungpulu Sayadaw, my robes were big, loose, baggy, and brown, symbolic of the forest.

There are thirteen extra austerities, or *dhutangas*, that monks may practice. It is said that women can take up only one of these austerities: the practice called "one meal, one bowl, at one sitting." When doing this practice, we can drink when we like, but eat only one meal a day, out of one big bowl, at one sitting. This practice completely changed my whole relationship to food and sustenance.

Since I was born on a Monday, I received the name Kuntulakati. Kuntulakati was first a Jain nun, a very feisty solitary wanderer. She had a stick, and as she walked around, she would place the stick in the ground as a signal that she would debate all comers. So, one day Shariputra challenged her to a debate, posing one question after another. Finally, she was unable to answer one of the questions and asked for clarification, so Shariputra took her to meet the Buddha. In this way she became a Buddhist nun and, like all Buddhist nuns in that day, she became enlightened. It is wonderful to read about the fantastic liberation experiences of the Buddhist nuns.

In Thailand, I lived with a Thai nun who has just recently died. She lived an incredibly simple life. Waking up very early in the morning, she meditated, and then, after cooking for herself and her dog, she continued to meditate the rest of the day. In the evening, she did standing meditation while listening to Buddhadasa's discourses over the loudspeaker, into the night. We lived in silence. Monastic life is usually either silent or what is called "noble silence," speaking only when necessary. The precepts pertain to actions of body, speech, and mind.

One quite endearing aspect of the monasteries, particularly in Burma, is that children ordain—a missing element in Western Buddhism. When I was in Burma, there were both boys and girls struggling to keep their robes on, trying to keep it over the shoulder, you know...no pushing in the lunch line. Then when I went to visit Burmese homes, the people would have pictures of their children and grandchildren when they were ordained. This is an incredible connection for children. In contrast, when Don Morales was doing his research on Buddhist centers and teachers for *Buddhist America*, he was unable to include a section on children and childcare, because there wasn't enough information. Something crucial is missing here.

When children came, and many did, to ordain at Thathana Yeitktha Monastery, they gained a wonderful sense of their connection with Buddhism. They learned what it means to take precepts and to be ordained. At a very early age, these children have the advantage of taking the precepts and having important values instilled—not to kill, not to step on the ants, not to hurt the turtles, and all the other things that kids might mistakenly think are fun. During the school breaks, children have the opportunity to ordain at the monasteries so that they can develop their awareness as human beings. This was also an opportunity for working women to choose ordination and participate in a three-month retreat during their vacation time. There is a great respect for Buddhism in Burma, and a real openness towards ordination and precepts which allows them to take that much time off work. Here in America, we get two weeks.

An eight-precept nun in Burma is called *tila shin*, which means "upholder of the precepts." A ten-precept nun, a forest dweller, is called *yetayma*. In Burma, as in Thailand, the elderly also ordain. The unfortunate side of this is that the temples for nuns in Thailand are like old-age homes. The fortunate side is that it provides an opportunity for the elderly to ordain and live simply at that phase of life.

The generosity that is an intricately interwoven part of the monasteries of Burma and Thailand is another thing that struck me deeply when I was ordained. Burma used to be a wealthy country with plenty of rice. Now they have less rice and of poorer quality, but the tradition of extraordinary generosity continues. I was offered things to eat or drink everywhere I went. Once, when I went to a very small monastery, the elderly head monk there chose to go out on alms rounds to collect food for me. People go to astounding lengths to support someone who has ordained and chosen to uphold the precepts and give their life to meditation. Having taken ordination, I was able to experience the extent of their generosity.

The Buddha talked about the relationship of the ordained person to the lay community. The ordained person has the responsibility of upholding the precepts, of maintaining meditation practice, and of truly receiving. There is an element of hierarchy involved, however, for it is considered better to give to an enlightened person or a monk or nun, because of their pure receptivity. But actually receptivity applies to everyone. Every time I received the people's generosity, I felt this openness.

One morning I was walking to the dining hall for my breakfast. I used to walk slowly, so I would start very early, before the sun rose. I saw a laywoman coming towards me and as I stopped, she went into a full prostration and then offered me paper money equivalent to about ten cents. The purity of her offering marked my entire day; that someone had that degree of devotion and generosity definitely made me mindful. That degree of support for spiritual practice is hard to find in Western society.

Monasticism involves both give and take. It's not that we renounce and hide, cutting ourselves off from the world, but rather that we create a very different relationship with others and the world. When I did the practice of *ekatani*—one meal, one bowl, one sitting—just receiving very simple food, I felt gratitude for all aspects of food. My training carries through even now while, as a mother, I cook three meals a day. When anyone offers me food, I have the deepest gratitude. Certain aspects of my monastic training have definitely carried over.

Response: Could you explain a bit more about temporary ordination?

Jacqueline: The monasteries of the Theravada tradition in Burma and Thailand allow for temporary ordination. There is also a monastery in Boulder Creek, California, where temporary ordination is given for women and men. People can even ordain for a weekend. Although other traditions may view it differently, it is common in Burma and Thailand to ordain temporarily and there is no stigma associated with disrobing, which is called "changing the precepts." For example, at one time I changed from the eight precepts to the five precepts and another time I changed from the ten precepts to the five precepts.

Response: Is temporary ordination available in Sri Lanka?

Sandy Boucher: I trained at a nunnery called Parappuduwa Nuns' Island in Sri Lanka, which was founded by a Western woman, Ayya Khema. Western women can go there for a three-month period during the "rains retreat" in summer. They take the eight precepts and then are free to leave if they wish. The point of the retreat is to provide a monastic setting within which to gain a deep experience of meditation. Because I live in Oakland, the experience of safety there was extraordinary for me. With no telephone and no electricity, there were no distractions except the roaches and the ants.

Response: Is temporary ordination also available in Mahayana countries?

Karma Lekshe Tsomo: In Mahayana Buddhist countries such as China, Korea, Tibet, and Vietnam, both novice and full ordinations, as well as lay ordinations, are taken for life. In these countries there is also a tradition of taking precepts for twenty-four hours, but that is a different category of ordination, because it is a temporary commitment. People take eight precepts and keep them from sunrise one day to sunrise the next day, devoting that day to practice and keeping an awareness of the precepts throughout the day. The tradition of taking precepts for twenty-four hours also exists in Theravada countries, such as Burma, Sri Lanka, and Thailand, the only difference being that in the Mahayana tradition, one takes them with the bodhicitta motivation.

Otherwise, in Mahayana countries the lay precepts, novice precepts, full precepts of bhikshu or bhikshuni, and bodhisattva precepts are all taken as lifetime commitments. Some Tibetan masters say that if you don't take the precepts with the intention to keep them for life, you don't really receive the ordination. I've also spoken with some monks in Sri Lanka and Thailand who say that they took ordination for life. This point needs to be clarified further. There may be different points of view even in Theravada countries. One Sri Lankan bhikshu told me that both options are available: you may take ordination either as a lifetime commitment or as a short-term commitment. People often get ordained to create merit, because it's said to be extremely virtuous to keep precepts even for a short time.[2]

Response: I would like to ask all of you how you made the choice to go into a monastic setting. And my question to Jacqueline is how did you make the choice not to continue in a monastic setting?

Jacqueline: I have some natural renunciate tendencies, so that was part of my decision to ordain. And one of my teachers, Taungpulu Sayadaw, really wanted me to continue being a nun, though I was free not to. When I ordained I hardly felt any different. My head felt lighter because it was shaved, but the robes felt perfectly natural. I just kept taking the next step in my practice. I felt like I wanted to go completely into all aspects of Buddhism and since Buddhism arose out of the monastic tradition and especially since I was teaching meditation, I wanted to do intensive practice as a nun. It was also an act of gratitude for me, to make the Buddha smile.

Response: Why did you leave?

Jacqueline: It's important to understand the different vision and commitment of the temporary ordination. For me it was a continuation rather than a leaving. I had meditated my entire adult life, usually within a monastery or meditation center. The choice to move on was one of wanting to fully explore other aspects of my life, to have children and fulfillment as a woman which, for me, was a total opening up of my body. It was a personal choice.

Sometimes people walk into my house and ask, "How can you live this simply?" Although I have chosen what is scripturally called a householder's life, I live more simply than I did at a meditation center. At the meditation centers I was often either teaching or involved in administration. I was always available and, of course, there were always politics. I have now restructured my life, along Western rather than Asian lines. As an adult, I am able to teach other adults without it being confused with a parent/child relationship.

Lekshe: I had a strong inclination toward contemplative life ever since I was a child. I was quite anti-social and my mother was really worried about me. It took me a long time to move into the world and learn to do all the things expected in American society. Buddhism and surfing were the only two things that made sense to me. I was totally disinterested in dating and all those sorts of activities, but growing up in California, I learned to go along with that way of life.

From the age of nineteen, I wanted to be ordained. On a ship from Yokohama to Singapore, I had a very clear dream of myself in robes, but I didn't know where to go. I never found a monastery for women in Asia. Maybe I hadn't experienced enough of life, because I went on to do just about everything—music, poetry, painting, aikido, tai chi, yoga, and a hundred other things—but I didn't find any real satisfaction in any of it. I wasn't interested in family life at all. I wanted to serve humanity at large, rather than a family. Still, it was thirteen years from the time of my original decision until I actually became ordained, with many adventures in between.

In brief, I got totally disheartened by intimate relationships. I found it very repetitive and tedious and just plain boring. I never felt comfortable wearing ordinary clothes. I had long blonde hair down to my waist, rings on every finger and toe. I wore every type of clothing—Japanese, Chinese, Filipino, American Indian, everything—but I never felt comfortable until I put on robes and chopped off my hair. It's not always easy being a Westerner in traditional Asian cultures, or a Buddhist nun in Western culture, but I definitely feel most comfortable being a nun. I think it has a lot to do with karma.

Eko Susan: It's very interesting to try and trace the important spiritual influences that lead one along the path. I was raised as a Roman Catholic. My grandmother was a very spiritual woman and my great-aunt was a Franciscan nun. I was quite a serious Catholic, drawn to the Catholic spiritual path, but as often happens with children who are raised as Catholics, as I grew intellectually, many questions arose. Young people often leave the Church because of certain problematic aspects of Catholic dogma.

I was genuinely searching spiritually when I encountered Buddhism. When I read Japanese literature in translation in high school, it was the Buddhist elements of Japanese culture I found most fascinating. This was a big awakening. While studying language and culture at a Japanese university in Tokyo, I began Zen practice at

Soji-ji Temple in Yokohama. When I returned to New York, although not actively searching for a spiritual teacher, I encountered the only Shingon priest in the United States who was actively teaching the Dharma to Americans.

Nora Ling-yun Shih: I used to work in a very competitive field, as a visual arts teacher. For a long time I had a feeling that something was missing in my life. I wanted to alleviate the sense of competition and tremendous pressure of my work, but I didn't know how. I never enjoyed dating. I never really liked drinking. I loved clothes, jewelry and all, but I liked to see them on others. I tried Transcendental Meditation and yoga, and thought that I needed to go in a spiritual direction, but I didn't know where to go or how. I liked being alone. It seemed that there were enough people in the world already, so there was no need for me to have offspring.

I was strongly attracted to Chinese culture and started studying Mandarin, then gave it up because it was so hard to learn. Because university departments are quite political and I felt that something was really missing, it suddenly occurred to me that I should do a different kind of work, so I left. I got a job taking care of convalescents and senior citizens, and found it extremely rewarding. All my colleagues told me that I had committed professional suicide, but I felt perfectly wonderful.

Then I found the Zen Center in Minneapolis and decided to try it. I did one sesshin after another and stayed for two years. There was something magnetic about Buddhism. The more I studied and practiced it, the more at home I felt within myself and in the world. I never really thought about becoming a nun. When the possibility came up to ordain in the Chinese tradition, I was really scared, so I decided to live as a lay nun for a year and work at a part-time job. From that time on, I wore clothes like everybody else, but my life was structured like a nun's. I love the simplicity. The precepts help me focus on what really matters in human life. I took the ten precepts and eventually the bhikshuni ordination. Monastic life has been so fragrant and luminous—as natural as breathing in and out.

Response: Eko Susan, you mentioned that you were married. How have you worked that out?

Eko Susan: I was married to a Japanese Shingon priest who was my first teacher. Our lives grew together in mutual commitment, but after we married it was clear that our relationship needed to evolve. He could not continue to be my teacher in a formal sense, nor could I be his student. I found that I still wished to continue my study of the Dharma and did so under a master at Mt. Koya. After that, my life changed profoundly. Although I do not think that a spiritual vocation is incompatible with marriage, I do think that it poses certain challenges, requiring flexibility and vision. In my particular case, it became clear that our paths were diverging and it became difficult for us to help each other further, so we divorced. My commitment to Dharma work and practice remains strong and I take great joy in that. At times we all face difficult decisions in creating a life situation which is most conducive to spiritual progress and service to others.

Chapter 13
Eastern Traditions in Western Lands

by Eko Susan Noble

When Buddhist women unite, they manifest the potential for spreading a wonderful light, for being conduits of the Buddhas' blessings. A flow of universal energy comes through our practice and we can use that flow of blessings to aid other beings who are suffering.

The purpose of all Buddhist practice is to realize enlightenment, to break down the duality: the sense of separateness between you and me, male and female, and so on. Ego and delusion keep us from realizing our interconnectedness with others; we think that we are very separate. Of course, on a conventional level we are individuals, but here it is crucial to understand how the Buddha distinguished conventional reality from absolute reality. In this lifetime, on a conventional level, we may be female, but the unborn knows no gender. As the *Mahavairochana Sutra* says, "The six great elements are interfused in a state of eternal harmony. I have realized that which is unborn. It is what language cannot communicate. It is free from all defilements. It transcends all causality. I know it is empty like space. I have gained the wisdom to see things as they really are. I am free from all darkness. I am the ultimately real and the immaculate."

Regarding practice, His Holiness the Dalai Lama gives this wonderful advice: "If you really take an interest in Buddhism, the most important thing is implementation: practice. To study Buddhism in order to use it as a weapon to criticize other theories and ideologies is wrong. The very purpose of religion is to control ourselves, not to criticize others. Rather we must criticize ourselves. How much am I doing about my anger, my attachment, my hatred, my pride, and my jealousy? These are things which we must check in daily life with the knowledge of the Buddhist teachings."

Buddhist practice gives us a way to purify our minds and to develop as much wisdom and compassion as we are capable of in this lifetime. Meditation can aid and inform us as we try to make a difference in the world. We must exercise great patience. Many times in my life, I have struggled desperately to go one direction or another. When I was twelve, I was perfectly convinced that I wanted to be an oceanographer. Then I wanted to be a geologist, a historian, and look where I ended up! Allen Ginsberg sings this funny little song: "I fought the Dharma and the Dharma won." So I would urge you not to feel confused. The Dharma has great plans for us all. We just have to be patient and cultivate skillful means until the time is right.

There are many in this world who take action with the best intentions. Buddhists realize intimately that there are certain things we can do to lessen the suffering of other beings. Children are dying, and many are hungry. Our responsibility as Buddhists is not only to address the immediate suffering on the conventional level, but to give beings the means to end their own suffering in absolute terms. Out of great compassion we can communicate to them these means as best we can, while traveling the very same path ourselves.

With very few exceptions, Buddhists don't proselytize. Buddhism recognizes that beginners must pass through different levels of development before they are able to hear the Buddhadharma. We all have the capacity, but some are not open to the teachings because of their karmic situations. Their path may be a different one and our efforts may not help. However, there are many who are ready to hear the Buddha's teachings, but may not have the good fortune to hear them. As Buddhists, we should be ready to teach by thought, word, and deed, with positive, loving energy.

We frequently speak about suffering, but we also need to talk about gratitude and humility. We need to develop profound gratitude for being able to encounter the Buddhist teachings and for having gained a human birth. Just having the opportunity of a human life gives us the potential for spiritual practice.

The all-pervasive mind of a Buddha knows every element of the universe. This concept is relevant to environmental issues. We need to clearly perceive the sacred nature of everything, including the unpleasant. A mind open to receiving teachings from all sources is a childlike mind—the beginner's mind of Zen. A child's mind is wonderful because it does not project. Children just look, feel, and take it all in without the reflective thinking and ego projections that can cause so much trouble.

The problem of ego and delusion cannot be addressed simply in terms of gender relationships. It is customary at women's gatherings to assume that men are largely responsible for the difficulties and inequality women face. But ego and delusion are common to all of us, whether we manifest in a male or a female body. They are not the exclusive preserve of any particular gender or nationality. I would like to relate a story that illustrates this point.

Soon after I arrived at Mt. Koya, the head nun, Takeuchi Sensei, was having some difficulty relating to me. I was not Japanese, but a "foreigner," which in Japanese literally means "a person outside." Takeuchi Sensei had lived through World War II and the defeat of Japan by America, but she was very proud of Japanese Buddhism and traditional culture. Encountering a real live American for the first time in forty-two years must have brought up interesting feelings for her. She naturally felt that being Japanese immediately connected one with the Buddhist tradition, and because I was not Japanese, she expected me to make mistakes. There was some confusion between nationality and being a Buddhist.

One evening Takeuchi Sensei launched into a discussion about karma and rebirth. She was lecturing the younger nuns who on that day had been particularly mischievous, though I was secretly grateful to them for providing welcome comic relief to balance the intensity of the training. She told them that they ought to be very grateful that they had been born as Japanese in this lifetime, graphically explaining the sufferings of people in other cultures, such as India. Then she said, "Just look at Susan. Even though she is an American, look how well she can chant the *Heart Sutra*. I think she must have been a Japanese in her past lifetime." Everyone nodded in agreement. There was the answer to the dilemma. Takeuchi Sensei had equalized the difference between the cultures. It didn't matter that in this lifetime I was a bumbling American, not intuitively understanding the nonverbal communication so prevalent in Japanese culture. I could be considered a part of the group because I had been a Japanese in my last life.

If indeed we can be reborn with different nationalities and genders in different incarnations, where does that leave our physical, generational ancestors? Some spiritual teachings place great emphasis on being reborn again and again in the same tradition. The Buddhist understanding is a lot more fluid. It recognizes that there are many currents of contributory karma. We have to deal with the karma of our actions in past lives and also with the collective karma of our physical ancestors of this present lifetime. For Buddhists, the karma of the present is most important, because past and future are manifestations of our minds.

Karma is very fluid and dynamic. The effects of our thoughts and intentions are sometimes even greater than our physical actions. Hindrances caused by our past karma can be cleared away, but the crucial thing is not to generate negative karma now. The law of cause and effect is absolutely fair. For every action, there is a reaction. We are responsible for ourselves and cannot blame others for our situation. Complaining will not improve our situation. We must work to clear away hindrances and generate merit, through good practice, such as meditation.

There are differences between Asian and Western approaches to Buddhadharma, especially in regard to form and content. For example, Tibetan monks and nuns usually memorize a text first and then proceed to study the content. I experienced a similar approach in Japan. First we were taught to dress in robes and behave like perfect Buddhist nuns, although we might be seething and egotistical in our hearts. But I realized that the outer form teaches and is a very important part of practice. Something in the sacred form communicates to us. Gradually something happens and the interior reality comes closer to the exterior appearance. Because the mind is very tricky, however, real progress cannot be made without a strong commitment to the practice. Sometimes it takes years, but the time is well spent.

Each of the various Buddhist traditions has developed methods to deal with the trickiness of the mind. But as therapists know, the human mind is ingenious and creative at avoiding confrontation with what is causing the suffering. Buddhist practice makes it more difficult to run away; we are challenged to examine our actions clearly. Sitting on our cushion and facing our true self requires discipline.

Discipline can bring great benefit and need not be militaristic, though in practicing both Shingon and Zen, I have sometimes felt like I joined the army. To be a little bit strict sometimes helps us progress spiritually. Everyone needs to find or create a fertile situation for practice and training. As the Dalai Lama says, "The most important thing is our daily life. We must be good honest persons. This is most important. We must sincerely practice what we believe.... Also, a beginner should not expect too much right from the beginning. Too much expectation will lead to failure. At the start you must realize that inner development will take time. It is not at all easy.... We must make strong determination to practice." Or, as Yamada Mumon Roshi puts it, "Anyone who attains the deadly earnestness of a cornered mouse can attain awakening."

This summer at a gathering of Native American elders in Vermont, a woman impressed me by saying that when we give away our power and our energy without fear, it returns to us in even greater force and merit. In the Buddhist tradition, too, we learn to give selflessly without expectations or thought of reward. On a conventional level, in order to survive, we receive sustenance and are part of a reciprocal exchange. Yet in the giving of energy and compassion, we experience the joy and happiness of the giving itself. The texts say, "The giver and the receiver are one."

One great gift is the giving of fearlessness: freedom from fear and aggression. We begin by ridding our own minds of fear: fear of other people, of being taken advantage of, of giving and not getting something in return. On a fundamental level, fear begins in our own mind. When we generate positive thoughts instead, we are treated differently by others.

America is a melting pot of nations and cultures. With a great tradition of eclecticism, we gather wisdom from many sources. In Buddhist cultures, we find a tradition of seeking guidance from a teacher or spiritual mentor. When we find a suitable teacher and an approach that rings true, we should follow that path as long as it is beneficial. The concept of faith in Buddhism is not blind faith in God or a deity, but faith to follow the path to goodness, insight, and enlightenment that others before us have tread. Buddhism has a long history of guiding in that direction.

We need to cultivate humility on the path. In Japan, humility is beaten into you, sometimes quite literally, through long years of hard practice. A Zen master named Hu Shan Nuang wrote to his friend: "One who is on the way but has not yet arrived, yet flashes learning and runs off at the mouth with intellectual understanding using eloquence and sharpness of tongue to gain victories, is like painting an outhouse vermillion. It only increases the odor."

Another master notes five important things we must understand: "What has been long neglected cannot be restored immediately. Ills that have been accumulating for a long time cannot be cleared away immediately. One cannot enjoy oneself forever. Human emotions cannot be just right. Calamity cannot be avoided by trying to run away from it. Anyone who has realized these five things can be in the world without misery." From my contact with Buddhism in Asia, I have learned that patience is necessary for spiritual progress, and the compassion we cultivate toward others should be directed to ourselves, too. We commit ourselves to conscious living and dedicate the merit to the benefit of others.

Continuing the Conversation

This book had its origins in a retreat for women held in California in August of 1989. At St. Mary's Seminary, in the sun-baked hills above Santa Barbara, forty women from North America met to explore together what Buddhism can offer women. The retreat in Santa Barbara was a forum for addressing these and other concerns surfacing in the minds of American Buddhist women. Our goal was to create a flexible structure, capable of meeting as many needs as possible. There was a mix of women, some of whom had been practicing for ten, twenty, or thirty years, and some who were brand-new to meditation, providing both depth and freshness, tradition and innovation.

A spirit of diversity pervaded the retreat. There were women from many different traditions: Theravada, Japanese Zen, Shingon, Chinese Pure Land, and various schools of the Tibetan tradition. There were women who had practiced in more than one tradition, some who were not affiliated with any particular tradition, and some who did not identify themselves as Buddhists. Rather than trying to establish a singular image, we rejoiced in our variety, consciously opening up to new and enriching experiences. Women from diverse backgrounds, with children and without, gathered together and discovered an empowering solidarity. Our intention was to learn from one another, to understand new ideas, and to hear one another's experiences of trying to live the practice day-to-day.

In response to participants' interests and expectations, the retreat began with prayers and a recitation of the *Heart Sutra*. After this, we gathered for meditation. We discussed formal meditation practice and its value, including the benefit of five concentrated minutes of meditation compared with an hour of mental wandering. All agreed, however, that formal practice alone is not enough— the challenge is to translate our practice into everyday life. How does our meditation practice influence the interactions we have with people and help us deal with everyday situations, like an angry bus driver or a domineering boss? How does it make us more congenial, constructive members of society? How does it help us develop patience while driving on the freeway, raising our children, or resolving difficulties with partners?

We began the program with an aspiration: "May whatever I do be for the benefit of living beings." Whether we call it a prayer or just a positive thought, this aspiration clarifies our motivation for spiritual practice. In the Mahayana tradition this is called the enlightened attitude, or bodhichitta. Starting off with this noble thought, the retreat became infused with the spirit of compassion, a process of healing ourselves as a contribution towards healing the world.

Tradition and Innovation

Asian Buddhist cultures have a keen interest in preserving tradition. It embodies everything they hold dear. American Buddhists have no similar stake in tradition. Their interests are preeminently pragmatic—an attitude of "take the best and leave the rest." American Buddhists see in the tradition elements of tremendous value, yet many refuse to be restrained within the confines of tradition. They are wary of the ritual and the religious overtones of Asian Buddhism, unaware that substance often follows form and discipline in a very beneficial way. They are also impatient for results. Accustomed to economic prosperity and instant gratification, there are few who are willing to wait for happiness or salvation in some future life. All of these factors are combining in the crucible that is embryonic American Buddhism.

Clearly, Buddhism is not a monolith. With its roots in India, it comprises many streams of thought, including many divergent philosophical points of view. This explains the difficulty in describing the phenomenon of Buddhism in America, which encompasses and draws from all these varied streams of thought. It is futile to claim any one point of view as being *the* authentic one, since all the traditions claim to be authentic and to have captured the essence of the Buddha's doctrine. Besides, claims to authenticity have a divisive effect and sectarianism is a feature of world religions we need not replay.

Ultimately, Buddhism comprises a rich feast of cultural, intellectual, and spiritual traditions, from which Americans may borrow at will. We have the option of studying with many great teachers, experiencing a wide variety of teaching techniques, corroborating our understanding with studies of the textual tradition, and verifying it through our own inner experience. Approached with an open mind, the more widely and deeply we study and observe this rich cultural feast, the greater our understanding and intuitive wisdom will grow.

Buddhist women in America are almost all "new Buddhists," at least new in this lifetime. Their words may lack some of the weight and depth of tradition, yet their viewpoint may be fresher, more personal, more dynamic. Buddhism today is merely one stream in a very rich and complex panorama of worldviews in American culture.

Ideas of consensus and equality have become cliches in the nineties in America. The tearing away of taboos and social circumscriptions, particularly when combined with the social fluidity bought with the currency of capitalism and the Pill, has had a profound effect on personal ethics. This, combined with egotism, clumsily disguised as individualism of the "me" generation, stands in diametric opposition to the selfless ethic of the bodhisattva.

America, as a society and as a culture, is very self-conscious and self-reflective. Here, in fact, we find ourselves self-consciously reflecting on our own experience of Buddhism. We may be premature in doing so, but don't we wish we knew how the first generation of Buddhists in China saw themselves as they accepted the teachings and other accompanying cultural components from India in the early centuries of this millenium?

The Buddha's words were meant to be tested and verified through one's own practice experience. The teachings presented by the women here have been heard, sifted through, digested, verified through personal experience, and applied in day-to-day life situations in recent years. We are not being asked to believe anything or accept anything (particularly not to buy something simply because a man said it, however enlightened he may have been). American women, having broken with a partriarchal path, are creating their direction, incorporating wisdom wherever they may find it.

Closing

A retreat is time away from our usual environment, our usual way of living and thinking. It enriches us and exposes us to new dimensions of experience. The retreat in Santa Barbara was an especially creative and rich blend of people and traditions, with an open sharing of meaningful ideas, philosophical views, personal experiences, meditations and other Dharma practices. Together we experienced a pilgrimage of the heart, visiting in imagination temples in India, Burma, and Japan to discover a vision of Buddhism's future in North America.

The closing ceremony was a time for sharing insights on how to creatively understand and apply our Buddhist practice to our lives in Western society. At an impromptu and eclectic altar, we offered incense to the Buddha, our spiritual forbearer and symbol of enlightened realization. Empowered by information, Dharma teachings, solidarity with like-minded friends, and feelings of joy and commitment, we resolved to share these blessings with our families, friends, teachers, and students. The image we took with us was an image of women full of the potential for enlightenment: positive, confident, compassionate, and capable of creating a genuine difference in today's challenging world.

Women today are continually discovering and reaffirming that women have tremendous energy for positive action. We want to join together and nurture that positive energy, then apply it to all our endeavors and relationships. Buddhist women are gaining a clearer idea of how to interweave Buddhist principles into everyday experience for the benefit of our troubled world. We are increasingly realizing the importance of using our energies wisely and supporting each other in wholesome spiritual development. In gatherings of genuine spiritual friends, we are learning to listen to each other better. This means letting go of all meaningless or self-defeating activities and empowering one another to work to our fullest spiritual potential.

The Buddhist teachings provide a refuge, a resource for dealing with the difficulties of life. Temporarily, attachment to the Dharma is all right. Dharma is our refuge, our life raft in the troubled sea of samsara, and we need to hang onto it until we reach the other shore.

At the end of the retreat, we expressed gratitude to everyone present. Gathering together in a circle, we intoned the refuge prayer together, chanted the "Om mani padme hum" mantra for the enlightenment of all beings, and made individual vows and aspirations. Chanting together, we made sincere offerings of the heart as we offered incense, resolving to implement the Dharma in a very personal way:

I vow to share. * I vow to recognize and to serve the Buddha in my husband and my daughters, as well as recognize the Buddha in myself. * I vow to begin to laugh at my anger, so that I may begin to follow the path. * To all the wonderful women here who have been teachers, I commit to have compassion for all humans and plants. * I vow to practice, to care, to explore, and to just do the best I can. * This day, I vow to experience the Buddha in everything—joy, sorrow, everything. I aspire to pause before I speak, to let me know my heart and let others know it, too. * I vow to seek the truth and to tell the truth, and to seek the truth some more and to tell the truth some more * I vow to maintain the warmth of all these humans beings. * I vow to serve all beings who come within my path and I vow to strive for enlightenment. * I aspire to teach. * I reaffirm my vow to the Sanctuary movement, to my friends in Central America. I aspire to be more joyful and more human. * I vow to work for the benefit of all. * I vow to gather courage in the power of the Dharma. * I vow to work for the welfare of others. * I vow to take responsibility. * I give thanks to the infallible wisdom of the Dharma. * I promise to purify myself for the sake of others. * I aspire to be kind and compassionate with myself and others. * I aspire to clarity. * I vow to develop compassion for the benefit of all beings every day. * I vow not to kill human beings now and in future lifetimes. I aspire to become completely non-violent and to help all beings be free from suffering. * I promise to work full-time for the benefit of beings, to the best of my abilities, for the rest of my life. * I reaffirm my bodhisattva vows. * I vow to abide in the spirit of universal offering to all sentient beings, that I may be a worthy vehicle for transmission of the Dharma. * The path to enlightenment is supreme. I vow to follow it. * I vow to save all beings. * I vow to work fully to help all beings find their paths to Buddhahood. I vow to serve those that are forgotten. I ask for guidance so that I may serve them more fully. * In this and all future lives, until I attain enlightenment, I promise to follow the path of the bodhisattva, to swiftly attain enlightenment, to lead all beings from the ocean of suffering to the bliss of enlightenment. *

Notes

Chapter 1
Forging a Kind Heart in an Age of Alienation

1. My own translation of Canto I, Verse 5.

2. *Buddha Vandana* (Los Angeles: Dharma Vijaya Buddhist Vihara, 1985), p. 27.

3. Maha Ghosananda, *Step by Step* (Berkeley: Parallax Press, 1992), p.27.

4. Slightly adapted from Kadampa Geshey Lang-ri-thang-pa, *The Eight Verses of Training the Mind* (Dharamsala: Secretariat of His Holiness the Dalai Lama).

5. Philip Kapleau, ed., *The Wheel of Death* (New York: Harper Colophon Books, 1971). In my opinion, this is the best and simplest guide to the dying process available to Westerners, and I deeply regret that it is out of print. A new volume by Kapleau, *The Wheel of Life and Death* (New York: Anchor Books, 1989), has a wealth of information about death and dying, but in my opinion is not nearly so simple and profound.

6. Ibid., pp. 80-81.

7. Thich Nhat Hanh describes this in *The Heart of Understanding: Commentaries on the Prajnaparamita Heart Sutra* (Berkeley: Parallax Press, 1988), p. 51.

8. Ibid., pp. 80-88.

9. Harold H. Bloomfield and Leonard Felder, *Making Peace with Your Parents* (New York: Ballantine Books, 1985), p. 16.

10. Thich Nhat Hanh, *Peace Is Every Step* (New York: Bantam Books, 1991), pp. 63-64, 59-60.

11. Ibid., p. 83.

12. Kapleau, p. 80.

Chapter 3
Reflections on Impermanence

1. H.H. the Dalai Lama, *Universal Responsibility and the Good Heart* (Dharamsala: Library of Tibetan Works and Archives, 1980), p. 140.

Chapter 8
Abortion: A Respectful Meeting Ground

1. For good resources on this subject, see the following books:

The Worst of Times by Patricia G. Miller (New York: Harper Collins, 1993).

Contains individual stories critical to understanding women's experiences.

Abortion: The Clash of Absolutes by Laurence H. Tribe (New York: Norton, 1990).

Presents the history of abortion in countries around the world, as well as in the United States. Supplies details rather than generalizations, making it easy to understand ourselves and our opponents.

The Choices We Made, ed. by Angela Bonavoglia (New York: Random House, 1991).

This book also abounds with important details and individual stories about what women do when they feel cornered and desperate. It is sometimes stunning to learn the extent of ignorance about sex, fertility and birth control.

Liquid Life: Abortion and Buddhism in Japan by William R. LaFleur (Princeton: Princeton University Press, 1992).

A fascinating look at abortion in Japan for Americans trying to find their own way on this issue. Although the Japanese experience may not be one we will want to replicate, understanding it should enhance our ideas about how to proceed here at home.

Soul Crisis by Sue Nathanson (New York: New American Library, 1989).

This is a remarkable and useful book. Nathanson, in revealing the particulars of her grieving and healing, suggests a way to be with ourselves in a compassionate and honest way. I strongly recommend this book.

Chapter 9
Buddhism and the Twelve Steps

1. Alcoholics Anonymous, *The Big Book*. Third edition. New York: Alcoholics Anonymous World Services, 1984. Available from Alcoholics Anonymous World Services, Box 459, Grand Central Station, New York, NY 10163.

2. "Prayers of Request to the Lady Tara who is Inseparable from the Guru, including all the Points of the Path." Translated by Carol Savvas and Lodro Tulku. In *Transformation into the Exalted State: Spiritual Exercises of the Tibetan Tantric Tradition* (Rikon-Zurich: Tibet Institute, 1987), p. 24.

Chapter 10
Karma: Creative Responsibility

1. Tenzin Gyatso, the 14th Dalai Lama, *The Meaning of Life from a Buddhist Perspective*. Trans. and ed. by Jeffrey Hopkins (Boston: Wisdom, 1992), p. 84.

Chapter 12
The Monastic Experience

1. The exact words from the sutra are: "Whatever monk should indulge in sexual intercourse is one who is defeated and no longer in communion."

2. According to Bhikkhu Tapowaneya Sutadhara, the tradition of temporary ordination was introduced to Sri Lanka around 1980 by Bhikkhu Nyanisera of Galaboda. Ordinarily, a person who wishes to become a monk approaches a *bhikṣu* (Pāli: *bhikkhu*) of at least five years' standing to request ordination. The teacher shaves the disciple's head, ties the robe around his neck, and then gives the ten precepts. The disciple recites: "I dedicate my life to the Buddha, Dharma, and Sangha. The ordination I receive today is the most precious thing in the world. I will protect the ordination received today for my whole life."

When one accepts the ten precepts (in a ceremony called *prabajja* in Pali), the precepts are considered inviolable and inextricably bound together such that if one is lost, all are lost (literally, "When you break one, the others get loose."). This point, however, is controversial. Some feel that it could be used by politicians to disrobe certain monks.

In the case of nuns, a *dasasila mātā* (literally, "ten precept mother") can wear robes without a teacher, while a *śrāmanerikā* (Pāli: *sāmanerī*, or novice nun) must take precepts with a teacher. In the Theravada countries, it is argued that the teacher who ordains a woman as a nun must be a *bhikṣunī* (Pāli: *bhikkhuni*, or fully ordained nun). In the Chinese, Korean, Tibetan, and Vietnamese traditions, it is considered allowable for *bhikṣus* to ordain a woman as a *śrāmanerikā*, since the ten precepts of a *śrāmanerikā* are the same as the ten precepts of a *śrāmanera* (Pāli: *sāmanera*, or novice monk).

Glossary

Avalokiteshvara (Skt: Avalokiteśvara) The bodhisattva (or Buddha) of compassion, who appears in numerous forms, some male and some female.

bhikshu (Pāli: *bhikkhu*; Skt: *bhiksu*) A fully ordained monk, who trains in over 200 precepts, including celibacy.

bhikshuni (Pāli: *bhikkhuni*, Skt: *bhiksunī*) A fully ordained nun, who trains in over 300 precepts, including celibacy.

bodhichitta (Pāli, Skt: *bodhicitta*) The enlightened attitude of wishing to achieve Buddhahood for the sake of all sentient beings.

bodhisattva (Pāli, Skt.) A being who has generated an unwavering resolution to achieve enlightenment for the sake of all sentient beings.

Buddha (Pāli, Skt.) An awakened, fully enlightened being; one who has eliminated all delusions and achieved all positive qualities.

Buddhahood The state of perfect enlightenment achieved by a Buddha.

Buddha nature The seed or potential to achieve perfect enlightenment.

Buddhadharma (Skt.; Pāli: *buddhadhamma*) The Buddha's teachings, or path to enlightenment taught by the Buddha.

Chenresig (Tib: sPyan ras gzigs) Avalokiteshvara, the bodhisattva of compassion. Chenresig appears in numerous forms in Tibet, the most popular being those with two arms, four arms, and a thousand arms.

Dalai Lama (Tib.) The spiritual and political leader of the Tibetan people. The term derives from a Mongolian title translated as "Ocean of Wisdom."

dasasila mātā (Pāli) A ten-precept nun of Sri Lanka.

dependent arising The theory that all phenomena arise in dependence upon causes and conditions.

Dharamsala A town in northern India where the present Dalai Lama resides and has established the Tibetan Government-in-Exile.

Dharma (Skt.; Pāli: Dhamma) The teachings or path taught by the Buddha to guide sentient beings in liberating themselves from suffering and achieving enlightenment.

Dharmagupta (Skt.) A school of Vinaya, or monastic discipline, currently practiced in China, Korea, and Vietnam. The only Vinaya school which has a living bhikshuni lineage.

dharmakaya (Skt: *dharmakāya*) The formless "truth body," or the enlightened realization, of a Buddha.

dhutanga (Pāli) A Buddhist ascetic practice.

Dzogchen (Tib. *rdzogs chen*) A tradition associated with the Nyingma school of Tibetan Buddhism which teaches resting the mind in its ultimate nature. Literally, "Great Completion" or "Great Perfection."

emptiness The lack of true or inherent existence of phenomena.

Guru Padmasambhava The Indian tantric master, also known as Guru Rinpoche, who established Buddhism in Tibet in the eighth century. Literally, "Lotus Born One."

Heart Sūtra A central Mahayana sutra, or text, on the nature of emptiness.

Jizō (Jpn.) Kshitigarbha Bodhisattva, who in Japanese tradition is a protector of women and children.

Jōdo Shinshū (Jpn.) The True Pure Land school of Japanese Buddhism, which centers on the practice of Amitabha Buddha, Buddha of Infinite Light.

kami (Jpn.) Deified forces of nature in Shinto, the indigenous Japanese religion.

karma (Skt.; Pāli: *kamma*) The law of cause and effect. Literally, "action."

Kshitigarbha (Skt: Kṣitigarbha) The "Earth Store" bodhisattva who in Japanese tradition is a protector of women and children.

Kuan Yin (Chin.) Avalokiteshvara, the bodhisattva of compassion. The form of Kuan Yin most frequently encountered in China is female, standing and holding a vase.

Kūkai (Jpn.) Founder of the Shingon school of Buddhism in Japan.

lama (Tib: *bla ma*) A teacher or spiritual master. Equivalent to the Sanskrit term "guru."

Madhyamika (Skt: *mādhyamika*) A Mahayana school of philosophical tenets which teaches emptiness as the "middle way" between eternalism and nihilism.

Mahayana (Skt: *mahāyāna*) Literally, "Great Vehicle." The Buddhist tradition prevalent in China, Japan, Korea, Mongolia, and Tibet, which accepts as authentic the Prajnaparamita texts.

mandala (Skt: *maṇḍala*) The abode of a tantric meditational deity or its visual representation; a psychocosmic diagram.

mantra (Skt.) Sound syllables, often associated with particular bodhisattvas and tantric meditational deities, which are visualized and recited in meditation practice.

meditation Contemplation, including concentration, visualization, analysis, and reflection on points of the teachings, and its application in action.

mudra (Skt: *mudrā*) Symbolic hand gestures associated especially with tantric meditation practices.

Om mani padme hum (Skt.) The mantra of Avalokiteshvara, Bodhisattva of Compassion.

nirvana (Pāli: *nibbana;* Skt: *nirvāṇa*) The state of liberation from suffering that is attained through eliminating attachment, aversion, and ignorance.

prajna (Skt: *prajñā*) Primordial wisdom, particularly the wisdom directly understanding emptiness.

precepts Guidelines for training in wholesome conduct to which a Buddhist commits voluntarily. There are five precepts for Buddhist laypeople: to refrain from killing, stealing, lying, sexual misconduct, and intoxicants.

Pure Land A school of Buddhism in China and Japan that centers around the practice of Amitabha. Also, the abode of a fully enlightened being.

Rinpoche (Tib.) A term of address for revered teachers, particularly recognized reincarnate teachers of the Tibetan tradition. Literally, "precious one."

sadhana (Skt: *sādhana*) A meditation practice involving ritual, visualization, invocation, and recitation of mantras.

Saichō (Jpn.) The founder of the Tendai school of Buddhism in Japan.

Sakyadhītā (Pāli) The Internation Association of Buddhist Women founded in Bodhgaya in 1987. Literally, "Daughters of the Buddha."

Shakyamuni (Pāli: Sakyamuni; Skt: Śākyamuni) The Buddha of the present historical era. Literally, "Sage of the Shakya clan." The Chinese assign a date of 949 B.C.E. to the Buddha's death, the Burmese put it at 622 B.C.E., modern scholars using Pāli sources propose 483 B.C.E., while modern Japanese scholars collating all sources propose 383 B.C.E. There is consensus that the Buddha lived for 80 years and was born near what is now the India-Nepal border.

samadhi (Pāli; Skt: *samādhi*) Meditative stabilization.

sāmanera (Pāli), *śrāmaṇera* (Skt.) A novice monk who trains in the ten precepts.

sāmanerī (Pāli), *śrāmaṇerikā* (Skt.) A novice nun who trains in the ten precepts.

shamata (Pāli; Skt: *śamatha*) Calm abiding, or single-pointed concentration.

samsara (Skt: *saṃsāra*) Cyclic existence, the process of birth, death, and rebirth.

Sangha (Skt: *saṅgha*) Literally, "virtuous assembly." Traditionally, the term refers to one or more Arya ("superior") beings, those who have achieved the Path of Insight and above. Conventionally, it denotes the monastic order, or an assembly of four or more monks or nuns. In North America is it frequently used to refer to Dharma practitioners in general.

Sanskrit An ancient literary language of the Indian subcontinent.

seiza Traditional Japanese style of sitting on the knees.

sentient being Living beings migrating within cyclic existence.

sesshin A period of intensive meditation practice in the Japanese Zen tradition.

Shingon The esoteric, or tantric, tradition of Buddhism in Japan founded by Kukai. Literally, "True Word."

shōgun (Jpn.) A "commander in chief"; one of a succession of rulers during the Tokugawa era in Japan.

shūso (Jpn.) "Head monk"; an official position in Japanese monastic organization.

siddha (Skt.) An accomplished practitioner.

sīla (Pāli; Skt: *śīla*) Moral precepts; a code of ethical conduct.

sutra (Pāli: *sutta;* Skt: *sūtra*) A text or portion of the Buddhist scriptures containing discourses and teachings of the Buddha.

takahatsu (Jpn.) Almsround.

taking refuge Seeking the protection and guidance of the Buddha, Dharma, and Sangha; traditionally, the mark of becoming a Buddhist.

tangaryō (Jpn.) A period of waiting at the gate for admission to a monastery in Japan.

tantra (Skt.) Specialized meditation texts and practices centered on deity yoga, or visualization of oneself as a particular deity.

Theravada (Pāli, Skt: Theravāda) Literally, "Vehicle of the Elders." The tradition of Buddhism prevalent in Burma, Cambodia, Laos, Thailand, and Sri Lanka, which relies on the Pali canon.

Three Jewels The three precious treasures: Buddha, Dharma, and Sangha.

tila shin (Bur.) A eight- or ten-precept nun of Burma (now Myanmar).

Vajrayana (Skt: Vajrayāna) Literally, "Adamantine Vehicle." The tradition of Buddhism utilizing tantric meditation texts.

Vipassana (Pāli; Skt: *vipaśyanā*) Literally, "insight." A realization; a method of meditation practice.

yetayma (Bur.) A ten-precept forest-dwelling nun of Burma.

Zen (Jpn.) A Japanese Buddhist school concerned with directly realizing the true nature of one's own mind. The counterpart of Chinese Ch'an and Korean Soen.

Further Reading

Books on Women in Buddhism

Allione, Tsultrim. *Women of Wisdom*. New York: Arkana, 1986.

Bartholomeusz, Tessa. *Women under the Bo Tree*. New York: Cambridge University Press, 1994.

Beyer, Stephan. *The Cult of Tara: Magic and Ritual in Tibet*. Berkeley: University of California Press, 1973.

Blakiston, Hilary. *But Little Dust*. Cambridge: Allborough Press, 1991.

Blofeld, John. *Bodhisattva of Compassion: The Mystical Tradition of Kuan Yin*. Boulder: Shambhala, 1978.

Boucher, Sandy. *Turning the Wheel: American Women Creating the New Buddhism*. San Francisco: Harper and Row, 1988.

Byles, Marie B. *Journey Into Burmese Silence*. London: George Allen & Unwin, 1962.

Cabezón, José Ignacio, ed. *Buddhism, Sexuality, and Gender*. Albany: State University of New York Press, 1992.

Chang, Pao. *Biographies of Buddhist Nuns*. Trans. by Li Jung-hsu. Osaka: Tohokai, 1981.

Dowman, Keith. *Sky Dancer: The Secret Life and Songs of the Lady Yeshe Tsogyel*. London: Routledge and Kegan Paul, 1984.

Edou, Jérôme. *Machig Labdron and the Foundations of Chod*. Ithaca, New York: Snow Lion Publications, 1995.

Friedman, Lenore. *Meetings with Remarkable Women: Buddhist Teachers in America*. Boston: Shambhala, 1987.

Galland, China. *Longing for Darkness: Tara and the Black Madonna.* New York: Viking, 1990.

Grimshaw, Anna. *Servants of the Buddha.* London: Open Letters, 1992.

Gross, Rita M. *Buddhism After Patriarchy: A Feminist History, Analysis, and Reconstruction of Buddhism.* Albany: State University of New York Press, 1993.

Havnevik, Hanna. *Tibetan Buddhist Nuns.* Oslo: Norwegian University Press, no date.

Hopkinson, Deborah, Michele Hill, and Eileen Kiera, eds. *Not Mixing Up Buddhism: Essays on Women and Buddhist Practice.* Fredonia, New York: White Pine Press, 1986.

Horner, I. B. *Women Under Primitive Buddhism.* London: Routledge & Kegan Paul, 1930 (reprint Delhi: Motilal Barnasidass, 1975).

Kabilsingh, Chatsumarn. *Thai Women in Buddhism.* Berkeley: Parallax Press, 1991.

Khong, Chan. *Learning True Love: How I Learned and Practiced Social Change in Vietnam.* Berkeley: Parallax Press, 1993.

King, Sallie B., trans. *Passionate Journey: The Spiritual Autobiography of Satomi Myodo.* Boston: Shambhala Publications, 1978.

Klein, Anne C. *Meeting the Great Bliss Queen: Buddhists, Feminists, and the Art of the Self.* Boston: Beacon Press, 1995.

Kunsang, Erik Pema. *Dakini Teachings: Padmasambhava's Oral Instructions to Lady Tsogyal.* Boston: Shambhala, 1990.

Law, Bimala Churn. *Women in Buddhist Literature.* Varanasi: Indological Book House, 1981.

Murcott, Susan. *The First Buddhist Women: Translations and Commentary on the Therigatha.* Berkeley: Parallax Press, 1991.

Norman, K. R., trans. *The Elders: Verses II: Therigatha.* London: Pali Text Society and Luzac and Company, 1971.

Paul, Diana. *Women in Buddhism: Images of the Feminine in Mahayana Buddhism.* Berkeley: University of California Press, 1985.

Rhys-Davids, Caroline. *Psalms of the Sisters.* London: Pali Text Society, 1948.

Sakya, Jamyang, and Julie Emery. *Princess in the Land of Snows: The Life of Jamyang Sakya in Tibet.* Boston: Shambhala, 1988.

Seneviratne, Maureen. *Some Women of the Mahavamsa and Culavamsa.* Colombo: H.W. Cave & Co., 1969.

Shaw, Miranda. *Passionate Enlightenment: Women in Tantric Buddhism.* Princeton, New Jersey: Princeton University Press, 1994.

Sidor, Ellen S. *A Gathering of Spirit: Women Teaching in American Buddhism.* Cumberland, Rhode Island: Primary Point Press, 1987.

Tsomo, Karma Lekshe, ed. *Sakyadhita: Daughters of the Buddha.* Ithaca, New York: Snow Lion Publications, 1989.

Tulku, Tarthang, trans. *Mother of Knowledge: The Enlightenment of Ye-shes mTsho-rgyal.* Berkeley: Dharma Publishing, 1983.

Willis, Janice D., ed. *Feminine Ground: Essays on Women and Tibet.* Ithaca, New York: Snow Lion Publications, 1989.

Willson, Martin. *In Praise of Tara: Songs to the Saviouress.* London: Wisdom Publications, 1986.

Introductory Books on Buddhism

Beck, Charlotte Joko. *Everyday Zen: Love and Work.* San Francisco: Harper and Row, 1989.

Chodron, Pema. *Start Where You Are: A Guide to Compassionate Living.* Boston: Shambhala, 1994.

Chodron, Thubten. *Open Heart, Clear Mind.* Ithaca, New York: Snow Lion Publications, 1990.

―――. *Taming the Monkey Mind.* Lutterworth, Leicestershire: Tynron Press, 1990.

Dalai Lama XIV, Tenzin Gyatso. *The Meaning of Life from a Buddhist Perspective.* Trans. and ed. by Jeffrey Hopkins. Boston: Wisdom Publications, 1992.

―――. *Kindness, Clarity and Insight.* Ithaca, New York: Snow Lion Publications, 1984.

Hanh, Thich Nhat. *Being Peace.* Berkeley: Parallax Press, 1987.

Hopkins, Jeffrey. *The Tantric Distinction.* London: Wisdom Publications, 1984.

Khema, Ayya. *Being Nobody, Going Nowhere.* London: Wisdom Publications, 1987.

————. *When the Iron Eagle Flies: Buddhism for the West.* London: Arkana, 1991.

Patrul Rinpoche. *The Heart Treasure of the Enlightened Ones: The Practice of View, Meditation, and Action.* Boston: Shambhala, 1992.

Rabten, Geshe and Geshe Dhargyey. *Advice from a Spiritual Friend.* London: Wisdom Publications, 1984.

Suzuki, Shunryu. *Zen Mind, Beginner's Mind.* New York: Tuttle, 1974.

Trungpa, Chogyam. *Cutting Through Spiritual Materialism.* Berkeley: Shambhala, 1973.

Contributors

Margaret Coberly is a registered nurse and a doctoral student in Transpersonal Psychology at the University of Hawai'i. She has been active in the hospice movement for more than ten years and is co-founder of a company that provides care for the elderly.

Bhikshuni Karuna Dharma is Abbess of the International Buddhist Meditation Center, a Vietnamese Zen Center in Los Angeles. She is the successor of Dr. Thich Thien-An, late Supreme Patriarch of the American Vietnamese Buddhist community.

Prabhasa Dharma Roshi did her monastic training in the Rinzai Zen tradition in Japan and has also been ordained in the Vietnamese tradition. She teaches and lectures widely both in Europe and the United States. She is founder and Director of the International Zen Center in Los Angeles.

Tsering Everest has been a student of H. E. Chakdud Rinpoche for fourteen years, and his translator for twelve years. Having completed a traditional three-year retreat, she now teaches extensively and gives empowerments in the Nyingma tradition.

Bhikshuni Ayya Khema is a meditation teacher of the Theravada tradition and the author of several books on Buddhism, including *Being Nobody, Going Nowhere* and *When the Iron Eagle Flies: Buddhism for the West*. She has been instrumental in founding Wat Buddhadharma in Australia, Parappuduwa Nuns' Island in Sri Lanka, and Buddha-Haus in Germany.

Michelle Levey has trained intensively in the Theravada and Tibetan traditions over the past twenty years. She is President of InnerWork Technologies, a Seattle-based consulting firm and has co-authored numerous books with her husband, including *The Fine Arts of Relaxation, Concentration & Meditation* and *Quality of Mind.*

Jacqueline Mandell is a senior teacher of Mindful Awareness Meditation and was authorized to teach by Ven. Mahasi Sayadaw. Her biography has been included in several volumes on women in Buddhism. She is the mother of twin daughters.

Eko Susan Noble is a teacher of the Shingon tradition. She trained at the Nuns' Training Institute on Mt. Koya, Japan, and was ordained as a priest in 1988. She is currently abbot of Daifuku Temple in Nara Prefecture.

Yvonne Rand is a Zen Buddhist priest and meditation teacher at a small center in northern California. As a teacher, she draws from her Buddhist training, her experiences as a wife and mother, and long-standing interests in Western psychotherapy, art, gardening, and literature. She has been involved in caring for the dying for many years.

Bhikshuni Nora Ling-yun Shih is an artist and experienced meditator practicing in the Chinese Ch'an tradition. She is currently in residence at Chung Hwa Meditation Center in New York.

Nancy Furyu Schroeder came to the San Francisco Zen Center in 1978 and received ordination there in 1986. She has served in all the monastic positions and is currently Director of Green Gulch Farm in Sausalito, California.

Heidi Singh is a meditation teacher, poet, wife, and mother. She was ordained as a lay minister at Dharmavijaya Vihara is Los Angeles and has served as Buddhist Chaplain at UCLA for several years.

Bhikshuni Karma Lekshe Tsomo is secretary of Sakyadhita: International Association of Buddhist Women and founder of Jamyang Chöling Institute for Buddhist Women in India. She is currently in the Philosophy Department at the University of Hawai'i.

Rachel V. is an experienced Buddhist practitioner, writer, and mother of three. She is author of *A Woman Like You*, stories of women recovering from alcohol and addictions, and *Family Secrets*, stories of adult children of alcoholics.

Index

AA (Alcoholics Anonymous) 93-95
abortion 85-89, 97, 101-02
Advice from a Spiritual Friend 37
AIDS 43, 48
alcoholism 91-96
Anandamaitreya, Balangoda 17
anger 66, 72, 98, 100, 102, 114, 159
appreciation 37
Avalokiteshvara 11, 27
awareness 41, 50, 51, 63, 65, 89, 141
Bateson, Gregory 93
bhikshu 122, 163
bhikshuni 122, 143, 164
Big Book, The 95
Bodhgaya 82
bodhichari 24
bodhichitta 53, 95, 143, 156
bodhisattva 24, 53, 74, 127, 136,
    157, 160
Bodhisattva, Jizo 85-88
Boucher, Sandy 143
Buddha nature 30, 96, 110, 115
Buddhadharma 85, 109, 111, 150,
    152
Buddhahood 11, 64, 107, 160
Burma (Myanmar) 53, 124, 138-43
Cambodia 16
cause and effect 98-99
celibacy 56-57, 122, 130, 131
Ch'an 136, 139
Chakdud Rinpoche 57, 112

children 47-59, 76, 97, 99, 101, 102,
    111
China 11, 26, 96, 135, 143
Chö 50
Coberly, Margaret 31-45
compassion 9, 15, 52, 54, 55, 85,
    100, 102, 103, 108-09, 111, 114,
    119, 124, 136
concentration 50, 63, 81
cyclic existence 97
Dalai Lama, His Holiness 16, 35,
    66, 101, 150, 153
dasasila mātā 164
death 17-23, 31-45, 54, 56, 85, 87,
    98, 108, 122
Dennison, Ruth 61
dependent arising 102
dependent origination 51
Dhammapada 15, 79
Dharamsala 66, 124
Dhargyey, Geshe Ngawang 37, 61-
    62, 123
Dharma, Bhikshuni Karuna 71-73
Dharmagupta 122
dharmakaya 25
dhutangas 140
Dickinson, Emily 31
Dipa Ma 49, 68
discipline 153
Discourse on Loving Kindness 15
dukkha 75-77, 82, 83, 84

Dzogchen 49, 50
effort 51, 109, 118
Eightfold Noble Path 78, 98
ekatani 142
enlightenment 11, 51, 80, 149, 159-60
equanimity 111
ethics 97-103, 138
Everest, Tsering 57, 105-19
faith 154
fear 33, 49, 65, 72, 87, 100, 110
Feminine Ground 139
Four Noble Truths 82
Gampopa 31
going for refuge 63-64
Ghosananda, Maha 16
Goenka, U.S.N. 98, 124
Green Gulch 135
grief 87
guilt 100
Hanh, Thich Nhat 23, 55, 58, 62
Heart Sutra 20, 21, 87, 123, 133, 152, 155
HIV 43
Hsi Lai Temple 135-38
humility 154
impermanence 31-45
intention 98, 99, 113, 115
Jamyang Chöling Institute for Buddhist Women 124
Japan 11
jealousy 111, 113
Jizo Bodhisattva 85-87
Jodo Shinshu 130
kami 130
Kapleau, Philip 19, 22
Karaniya Metta Sutta 15
karma 9, 30, 39, 52, 97-103, 109-11, 115, 145, 150, 152
Karmapa, Gyalwa 124
Khema, Ayya 75-84, 143
koan 47
Korea 11, 124, 129, 135
Koya, Mt. 125-28, 131, 145, 151
Kuan Yin 11, 27
Kukai 129

Lama Foundation 50
Lamrimpa, Gen 66-67
Levey, Michelle 58, 61-69
liberation 11, 38, 97, 98
Library of Tibetan Works and Archives 123
Longaker, Christine 94
love 66, 83, 102, 113, 119
loving kindness 17, 48, 67-69, 102
Madhyamika 62
Mahavairochana Sutra 149
Mahayana 10, 11, 57, 136, 143
Making Peace with Your Parents 23
mala 47
Mandell, Jacqueline 47-59, 138-44
mantra 56, 159
Marpa 55
meditation 21, 47-53, 57, 63-66, 72, 81-84, 98, 118, 127, 140, 152, 155
merit 116, 118, 152
mindfulness 36, 50, 78, 81, 98, 99
monasticism 121-47
monks 121-22, 130-31, 136, 152, 163
morality 9
motherhood 111
mothering 47-59
motivation 102, 114, 156
Myanmar (Burma) 53, 124, 138-43
Nepal 123, 135
nirvana 98
Noble Eightfold Path 98
Noble, Eko Susan 56-57, 58, 125-32, 145-47, 149-54
Nuang, Hu Shan 154
nun 121-47, 152-53
nun, eight-precept 141
nun, ten-precept 141
Nyanisera, Bhikkhu 163
Om mani padme hum 28, 56, 159
ordination 24, 126, 129, 141, 163
ordination, bodhisattva 136
ordination, full 124
ordination, novice 124, 127
ordination, priest 135
ordination, temporary 142-44, 163

ordination, ten-precept 139
Padmasambhava, Guru 106
Parappuduwa Nuns' Island 143
patience 124, 154
peace 105, 107-08
prabajja 163
prayer 159
precepts 88, 121-22, 129, 134, 139, 141
precepts, bhiksu 143
precepts, bhiksun 143
precepts, bodhisattva 130, 136
precepts, five 100-01, 115
precepts, eight 136, 138-39, 141, 143
precepts, Mahayana 19, 143
precepts, monks' 121-22, 129
precepts, novice 127, 143
precepts, nuns' 121-22
precepts, tantric 130
precepts, ten 138-39, 163
precepts, twenty-four-hour 136
preconceptions 118
pregnancy 52, 56, 57, 86, 87, 88, 101
Pure Land 136-37
purification 81
Rabten, Geshe 37
Rand, Yvonne 57, 85-89
rebirth 11, 38, 97, 151-52
reconciliation 15-23
refuge 61
rejoicing 113
relationships 17, 26, 66, 71-73, 158
renunciation 123, 139
responsibility 39-40, 97, 150, 159
retreat 49, 50, 51, 55, 57, 59
Rinpoche, Kalu 124
Rinpoche, Sogyal 94
Rinpoche, Jetsun Lochen 139
Roshi, Prabhasa Dharma 25-30
Roshi, Shunryu Suzuki 86, 132
Roshi, Yamada Mumon 153
Saicho 129
samsara 59, 115, 117, 118, 122, 159
San Francisco Zen Center 132

Sangha 63, 64, 94, 100
Santa Barbara 155
Sayadaw, Mahasi 138
Sayadaw, Taungpulu 139-40
Schroeder, Nancy Furyu 132-35
seiza 128
selflessness 98, 100, 109, 110, 115
Sensei, Bernie Glassman 94
Sensei, Takeuchi 151
sentient being 11, 100
separation 35, 42
sexuality 87, 89, 100, 121
Shakyamuni Buddha 25, 26, 67
shamata 63
Shariputra 140
Shih, Bhikshuni Nora Ling-yun 135-38, 146
Shingon 58, 125-29, 132, 145, 155
Shinran 130
Shinto 130
Shobogenzo 24
shogun 130
shuso 135
Singh, Heidi 15-23
śrāmaṇera 164
śrāmaṇerikā 164
Sri Lanka 17, 22, 143-44, 163
stress 75-84
suffering 12, 20, 51, 54, 75, 88, 89, 108-09, 111, 119, 124, 151
Sutadhara, Bhikkhu Tapowaneya 163
Taiwan 124, 135
takuhatsu 131
tangaryo 133
tantra 63, 132
Tara 11, 105-07, 163
Tassajara Monastery 54, 57, 86, 133-35
ten virtues 100
Tendai 129
terminal illness 18, 38, 97
Thailand 53, 140-43
Thatnana Yeiktha Meditation Center 139, 141

Tibetan Book of the Dead, The 35
Theravada 10, 11, 24, 68, 142-44, 155
theri 13
Three Jewels 63, 64, 100, 107
Tibet 38, 96, 143
Tibetan Buddhism 36-39, 61, 105,
    124, 155, 163
tila shin 141
Tokugawa 130
training, bodhisattva peace 105-19
transformation 9, 43, 134
Tsomo, Bhikshuni Karma Lekshe
    97-103, 121-25, 144-45
twelve steps 91-96
*Universal Responsibility and the Good
    Heart* 34
V., Rachel 91-96

Vajrayana 10, 11, 94, 132
Vesak 24
Vietnam 11, 137
Vipassana 61, 63, 137
visualization 64
vows 116
vow, refuge 109
vows, bodhisattva 22, 136, 160
Wheel of Death, The 19, 22
wisdom 98, 106, 118
Yeshe, Lama 59
yetayma 141
zazen 91, 94
Zen 18, 26, 29, 30, 57, 61, 85, 92, 94,
    126, 132-35, 145, 151, 155
zendo 92